JUST COURAGE

God's Great Expedition
for the Restless Christian

Gary A. Haugen

IVP Books

An imprint of InterVarsity Press
Downers Grove, Illinois

InterVarsity Press
P.O. Box 1400, Downers Grove, IL 60515-1426
www.ivpress.com
email@ivpress.com

InterVarsity Press® is the book-publishing division of InterVarsity Christian Fellowship/USA®, a movement of students and faculty active on campus at hundreds of universities, colleges and schools of nursing in the United States of America, and a member movement of the International Fellowship of Evangelical Students. For information about local and regional activities, write Public Relations Dept., InterVarsity Christian Fellowship/USA, 6400 Schroeder Rd., P.O. Box 7895, Madison, WI 53707-7895, or visit the IVCF website at <www.intervarsity.org>.

In order to protect the individuals that IJM serves and those who carry out the work, pseudonyms have been used for victims of sex abuse and for IJM investigators though the accounts are real. Actual names and casework documentation are on file with IJM.

All Scripture quotations, unless otherwise indicated, are taken from the Holy Bible, New International Version®. NIV®. *Copyright ©1973, 1978, 1984 by International Bible Society. Used by permission of Zondervan Publishing House. All rights reserved.*

Design: Cindy Kiple
Images: compass on woodgrain: Irochka_T/iStockphoto
person standing atop a mountain ledge: azgek/iStockphoto
paper texture: abzee/iStockphoto

ISBN 978-0-8308-4462-3 (paperback)
ISBN 978-0-8308-3494-5 (hardcover)
ISBN 978-0-8308-7592-4 (digital)

Printed in the United States of America ∞

Library of Congress Cataloging-in-Publication Data

Haugen, Gary A.
Just courage: God's great expedition for the restless Christian /
Gary A. Haugen.
p. cm.
ISBN 978-0-8308-3494-5 (cloth: alk. paper)
1. Boredom—Religious aspects—Christianity. 2. Christian life. I.
Title.
BV4599.5.B67H38 2008
248.4—dc22

2008008908

P 25 24 23 22 21 20 19 18 17 16 15 14 13 12 11 10 9 8 7 6 5 4 3 2

Y 38 37 36 35 34 33 32 31 30 29 28 27 26 25 24 23 22 21 20 19 18 17

Dedicated to Bob Mosier,

who chose to be brave.

Contents

Going on the Journey
but Missing the Adventure

EVEN THOUGH I READ THE WORDS ALMOST twenty-five years ago, I can still picture them upon the page. The words were and have remained so disturbing to me that I remember exactly where I was when I read them. I was a freshman in college sitting up late one night in the dorm laundry room waiting for my clothes to dry and reading John Stuart Mill's essay "On Liberty." Writing in 1859, Mill was trying to explain the process by which words lose their meaning, and he casually offered that the best example of this phenomenon was Christians. Christians, he observed, seem to have the amazing ability to say the most wonderful things without actually believing them.

What became more disturbing was his list of things that Christians, like me, actually say—like, blessed are the poor and humble; it's better to give than receive; judge not, lest you be judged; love your neighbor as yourself, etc.—and examining, one by one, how differently I would live my life if I actually believed such things. As Mill concluded, "The sayings of Christ co-exist passively in their minds, producing hardly any effect beyond what is caused by mere listening to words so amiable and bland."

Looking at each of the glorious declarations on the list and at the corresponding mediocrity of my own daily character, Mill's observation seemed simply and clearly true. What ended up surprising me, however, was what followed—which was not a rush of guilt or despair, but the opening of a fresh and unexpected window of hope. Perhaps my life need not be, in fact, so manifestly shriveled and mediocre if I began to act as if what Jesus said were actually true.

Christians, he observed, seem to have the amazing ability to say the most wonderful things without actually believing them.

Sometimes the teachings of Jesus are hard to believe, and sometimes they are simply hard to understand. One of his teachings that has always been nice to read but difficult for me to understand is the sweet Gospel vignette of Jesus admonishing his disciples for failing to see the value of children, saying, "Let the little children come to me," and declaring, "the kingdom of God belongs to such as these" (Luke 18:16).

If ever a teaching of Jesus qualified for the designation "amiable and bland," and threatened to have no discernible effect upon me at all, perhaps this is it. On the other hand, over time, I have found Jesus saying something in this story that has the power to utterly change my life. That is, if I were to live as if what he said were actually true.

Here then is the story.

People were bringing little children to Jesus to have him touch them, but the disciples rebuked them. When Jesus saw this, he was indignant. He said to them, "Let the little children come to me, and do not hinder them, for the kingdom of God belongs to such as these. I tell you the truth, anyone who will not receive the kingdom of God like a little child will never enter it" (Luke 18:16-17). And he took the children in his arms, put his hands on them and blessed them.

What does Jesus mean when he says we will never enter the kingdom of God unless we receive it like a child? And how would it change our lives if we lived as if this were true?

First, let's establish what it does not mean. *Receiving the kingdom of God* in Jesus' teachings does not mean simply receiving the salvation of the life hereafter. It certainly does include that, but it also means receiving and living in the kingdom and rule of God *now*. As Dallas Willard has described well:

> New Testament passages make plain that this kingdom is not something to be accepted now and enjoyed later, but something to be *entered* now; it is something that already has flesh and blood citizens who have been transformed into it and are fellow workers in it.

The *complete* rule of God's kingdom is, indeed, something yet to come, but Jesus continually beckoned his followers to enter daily into his rule and reign. And as earnest Christians, you and I are rightly yearning to walk in the way of Jesus, to experience the intimate presence of almighty God, to live daily in a completely different way because we know Jesus. In a word, we want to live *alive* to God.

This, I think, is what we all want. But how do we get to live like that? The answer, says Jesus, is by coming to him like a little child.

COME AS A CHILD

How does a child come to Jesus? To be straight and plain about it—a child comes in weakness, vulnerability and neediness. You come to experience my rule, my presence, my power, my life, Jesus says, when you come in the weakness and vulnerability of a child. Jesus makes this more explicit in Matthew 18, where it says:

> He called a little child and had him stand among them. And he said: "I tell you the truth, unless you change and become like little children, you will never enter the kingdom of heaven. Therefore, whoever humbles himself like this child is the greatest in the kingdom of heaven." (vv. 2-4)

Here, of course, is where the whole thing becomes difficult for me—and maybe for many of us.

I don't like to be weak, vulnerable and needy.

In fact, my initial response is denial: "Well, I'm sure this is a very encouraging verse for those who *are* weak, vulnerable and needy—and it's jolly good that Jesus is on their side." But I like to believe that my friends and I are cut out for more a muscular approach to the life in Christ.

On the other hand, I know Paul teaches in 2 Corinthians 4 and 12 that God's power is made perfect in my weakness, that the power of Christ actually dwells in me in my manifest weakness, that my weakness is actually meant to show that this all-surpassing power is from God and not from me, and that "when I am weak, then I am strong."

Of my belief in these familiar passages, Mill wrote 150 years ago:

[Christians are] not insincere when they say that they believe these things. They do believe them, as people believe what they have always heard lauded and never discussed. . . . They have a habitual respect for the sound of them, . . . [but] whenever conduct is concerned, they look round for Mr. A and B to direct them how far to go in obeying Christ.

And how far do I go? To be brutally honest, as far as I am safe. As far as I am in control. As far as the risks feel manageable. As far as my sphere of certain competence will take me.

And consequently, in my secret and most honest moments, I sense it doesn't take me very far at all.

THE PARADISE VISITOR'S CENTER

One of the biggest regrets of life, I think, is a sense of having gone on the trip but missed the adventure. One summer when I was ten, I was camping and hiking with my dad and two older brothers on Mount Rainier, a massive volcanic dome of rock and glaciers rising 14,410 feet into the clouds outside Seattle. The mountain creates its own weather, still steals the lives of scores of climbers and served as the training mountain for the first American team to scale Mount Everest. Below the tree line is one of the nation's oldest and most dramatic rain forests, with its absurdly giant Douglas fir trees. Visitors to the park can drive up to a breathtaking alpine meadow called Paradise, which averages more than fifty feet of snow during the winter and arguably has the world's most spectacular display of alpine wildflowers during the summer.

One of the ways my father expressed his love for us was to take us to such places and to simply walk—mile after mile—up into the beauty and grandeur of these sacred treasures. My older brothers would race up the trail to the next dramatic vista, leaving me behind—struggling. But Dad would always stay with me, making me feel like I was setting the pace and enjoying, I think, the sweetness of being with his little boy in the quiet of the massive mountain. We always went farther and higher than *I* would have chosen. But along the way, Dad was there—to steady me over streams, to feign the need for a rest, to help me over the boulder, to assure me I was almost there.

But on this particular summer day I didn't want to go on. We had been walking with hordes of tourists along the gentle asphalt trails outside the Paradise visitor's center, admiring and naming the fabulous wildflowers. At the top of the meadow trails, however, the paved trail ended and a large warning sign indicated the beginning of the trail used by climbers on their way to the summit. With a text undoubtedly drafted by lawyers, the sign warned of every conceivable horror that awaited those who ventured beyond. I wasn't feeling particularly tired, but my little stomach ached as I looked up at the massive rock formations and snow fields that went up and up and up. My dad suggested we try to reach Camp Muir, the base camp used by climbers heading for the summit, and my brothers eagerly accepted. Dad assured me I could make it, that he would help me and that the view and the triumph would be more than worth the effort—and that it would be marvelous to do together.

I, however, was thinking that we ought to pay more attention to the lawyers who took the time to make that nice sign. After all, all manner of things could go wrong. *What if Dad is wrong and I can't make it? It will be so humiliating to be the one who needs help again. And what if Dad doesn't even know the way up there? What if it becomes too aggravating for him to help me, and I get stuck?*

With these mounting anxieties beating in my little chest, I responded the only way a ten-year-old can to such a proposition and simply said:

"No. That looks boring."

Instead, I suggested, I'd like to hang out at the visitor's center. Indeed, the Paradise meadow had a huge and magnificent visitor's center with exhibits and video displays about the wildlife, the history of the mountain, the drama of those who had tried to climb it, and even a wildflower quiz for kids that I was sure I could win.

Dad tried a few more times to woo me up the mountain and explained that it would be a long day by myself at the visitor's center while he and my brothers were climbing, but eventually he relented. I scurried back down to the visitor's center and was quite pleased with myself while they headed up the mountain.

The visitor's center was warm and comfortable, with lots of interesting things to watch and read. I devoured the information and explored every corner, and judging by the crowd, it was clearly the place to be. As the afternoon stretched on, however, the massive visitor's center started to feel awfully small. The warm air felt stuffy, and the stuffed wild animals started to seem just—dead. The inspiring loop videos about extraordinary people who climbed the mountain weren't as interesting the sixth and seventh times, and they made me wish I could be one of those actually climbing the mountain instead of reading about it. I felt bored, sleepy and small—and I missed my dad. I was totally stuck. Totally safe—but totally stuck.

After the longest afternoon of my ten-year-old life, Dad and my brothers returned flushed with their triumph. Their faces were red from the cold and their eyes clear with delight. They were wet from the snow, famished, dehydrated and nursing scrapes from the rocks and ice, but on the long drive home they had something else. They had stories and an unforgettable day with their dad on a great mountain. I, of course, revealed nothing, insisting that it was my favorite day of the whole vacation.

Truth be told—I went on the trip and missed the adventure. And thirty-four years later, I still remember the day at the visitor's center.

STUCK AT THE VISITOR'S CENTER

Likewise, it is my sense that many Christians are starting to suspect that they are stuck at the visitor's center. They suspect that they are traveling with Jesus but missing the adventure.

In different times and in different ways, our heavenly Father offers us a simple proposition: Follow me beyond what you can control, beyond where your own strength and competencies can take you, and beyond what is affirmed or risked by the crowd—and you will experience me and my power and my wisdom and my love.

> Many Christians are starting to suspect that they are stuck at the visitor's center.

Jesus beckons me to follow him to that place of weakness where I risk the vulnerability of a child so that I might know how strong my Father is and how much he loves me.

But truth be told, I would rather be an adult. I'd rather be in a place where I can still pull things together if God doesn't show up, where I risk no ultimate humiliation, where I don't have to take the shallow breaths of desperation.

And as a result, my experience of my heavenly Father is simply impoverished. If I want to stay safe and warm at the visitor's center, I don't get to be with him on the adventure up the mountain. But he says his power is made perfect in my weakness, not in my strength.

Does this mean I need to abandon the things I do well? Do I have to let go of my sources of strength—my gifts, my passions, my training, my expertise? No, I don't think so. Those are good things from God. I think he simply wants us to take them on a more demanding climb, where we will actually need his help, and where he delights to grant it.

My difficulty is I either would prefer not to desperately need his help, or I would desperately like his help with things that aren't necessarily of *his* kingdom. (They are, instead, the things of *my* kingdom.) In both cases, my Father can't pour himself out in power because I'm either not asking for it or it would be bad for me. So I'm stuck at the visitor's center.

This is why I am so grateful for my experience with International Justice Mission (IJM)—because it gives me a continual experience of my weakness in which God is delighted to show his power. We are a collection of Christian lawyers, criminal investigators, social workers and advocates. We rescue victims of violence, sexual exploitation, slavery and oppression around the world. I started out as its first employee in 1997, and now we have about three hundred full-time staff around the world, most of whom are nationals working in their own communities in the developing world.

The journey for me has been incredible, but by far the most joyful, exhilarating and life-altering part has been the authentic experience of God's presence and power. I have experienced God—and that experience has come in my weakness. God has called us into a battle with violence and aggressive evil that, every day, my colleagues and I *know* we cannot win without the specific intervention of God. We are forced by our own weakness to beg him for it, and at times we work without a net, apart from his saving hand. And we have found him to be real—and his hand to be true and strong—in a way we would never have experienced strapped into our own safety harnesses.

In concrete terms, what does that desperation look like? For me, it means being confronted with a videotape of hundreds of young girls in Cambodia being put on open sale to be raped and abused by sex tourists and foreign pedophiles. It means going into a brothel in Cambodia as part of an undercover investigation and being presented with a dozen girls between the ages of five and ten who are being forced to provide sex to strangers. It means being told by everyone who should know that there is nothing that can be done about it. It means facing death threats for my investigative colleagues, high-level police corruption, desperately inadequate aftercare capacities for victims and a hopelessly corrupt court system. It means going to God in honest argument and saying, "Father, we cannot solve this," and hearing him say, "Do what you know best to do, and watch me with the rest." In the end it means taking that risky bargain and seeing

God do more than I could have hoped or imagined—setting girls free, providing high-quality aftercare, bringing the perpetrators to justice, shutting down the whole nasty operation, training the Cambodian authorities to do this work themselves and seeing the U.S. government be willing to pay for it.

DESPERATE NEED

In taking on the forces of aggressive evil, we have found a place where we desperately need our Father's help, and where he is delighted to provide it. This is not a resignation of my gifts or passions or training, but a deployment of those endowments to a place beyond safety, beyond my ability to control the outcome and beyond my own power to succeed. It's a place where God is desperately needed and a work in which he delights to engage— for it is his own work.

My colleague Sharon found herself in such a place not long ago when she and her colleagues were confronted with a man who was too strong for them. He was a powerful, notorious and ruthless slave owner in South Asia. When some of his slaves ran away—including a young father named Shiveraj—the slave owner sent thugs to kidnap Shiveraj's relatives from a distant village. They held them as hostages and savagely beat them as a way to force Shiveraj and the other slaves to return. IJM received the case and attempted a rescue operation with local police, but mistakes were made that risked a tip-off to the slave owner and possibly lethal retaliation against the hostages. Riding out to attempt rescue, Sharon's IJM colleagues discussed what they thought the chances were for success. One of the most experienced local staff members pegged the odds at about 3 percent—and then added, "but with God, 3 percent can become a majority."

Indeed, the God of justice was pleased to move on that day, and a series of utter miracles allowed the IJM team and local authorities to rescue all of the hostages and secure the release of the slaves. Sharon found the extravagant expressions of gratitude from the hostages to be one of the most overwhelming experiences of her life.

Sharon has not resigned her gifts and expertise as a Harvard-trained lawyer who once served with the Department of Justice's witness-protection program and as a litigator with an elite corporate law firm. Rather, she has intentionally taken those gifts onto battlefields where she knows she cannot win on her own, and where she believes God is pleased to stand with her. And she gets to experience God. Not without struggle and scrapes and doubts. But at the end of the day her cheeks are flushed, her eyes are clear, and she has stories. She has unforgettable days with her Father on great mountains.

But it's not just my IJM colleagues who have such days—nor just people who work in Christian ministries. I know a screenwriter and movie producer who has taken his craft into a battle for truth, beauty and authenticity that he cannot win on his own. He has cried out to God in weakness and has a blockbuster to show for it as well as a large collection of heartbreaks. But he has stories and unforgettable days with his Father on great mountains. Likewise, I've seen a friend imprudently give away millions to the work of God's kingdom in good days, and I've seen his business collapse in bad days. But coming or going—he's never found loitering in the visitor's center. He's on the high mountain. Though he's on the mountain as a child—his Father is with him.

Another godly friend is setting aside time to care for her elderly father, while another has taken a season to make his wife's academic pursuit the family priority. In each case, they are in over their heads and they won't make it without God, and that's exactly where they want to be—because they live like they believe that God's power is actually made perfect in their weakness.

The Source of Abundant Life

How do we find that abundant, heroic life for which we were made? How do we enter in to God's kingdom now and experience the authentic power and presence of God?

We do it in weakness, and we are comfortable with (and even boasting in) our weakness because we actually believe that our heavenly Father is both all-loving and all-powerful—and that all is well as long as we are with the One who neither leaves us nor forsakes us.

Accordingly, I can take my gifts and passions and training and strengths beyond the places of safety and control, and into the sphere of the kingdom where I actually need God.

Perhaps the first indicator that I am approaching such a place will be seen in my life of prayer. Mother Teresa said that she couldn't imagine doing her work for more than thirty minutes without prayer. Do you and I have work that we can't imagine doing for thirty minutes without prayer?

If not, perhaps we need a new life's work. Or perhaps we need to do an old life's work in a new way.

I won't need to be in prayer every thirty minutes in my work if I don't really need God's power to get it done, or if it's work that God doesn't really need done because it has nothing to do with his kingdom.

At IJM, we begin every working day with thirty minutes of silence and prayerful preparation for the day, and then we all gather again for prayer at 11 a.m. We don't do this so much as a matter of discipline but out of desperation. We don't think we can do the mission God has called us to or love each other the way we ought to without spiritual resources accessed through prayer.

When we are following our Father on the great mountain, we want and need to talk to him. It's natural. It's part of the journey. At the visitor's center, though, there are enough things to occupy us that such conversation really isn't necessary—checking in every once in a while is generally quite adequate.

But I don't think we really want to spend our days at the visitor's center. To get out, however, we have to admit that it's fear and not cleverness that's keeping us there. We need to believe that the Father really does know where the joy is, and that it's safe to follow him in our own weakness up the mountain. Perhaps then we can know the joy of going on the trip without missing the adventure.

From Rescued to Rescuer

JIM RAYBURN, THE FOUNDER OF YOUNG LIFE, a nationwide youth ministry, used to say, "It's a sin to bore a kid with the gospel." But what about adults? Is it okay to bore grownups with the gospel?

I ask the question because I sense among many Christians today a subtle but deep discontent. I don't think they would call it boredom because that sounds too flippant, but I do sense a powerful but largely unspoken sense of disappointment in the way their Christian life is turning out. And not because of failure, either. On the contrary, they are successful dads, passionate and gifted moms, accomplished professionals, mature friends, winsome small-group leaders, respected elders, diligent students, and loving neighbors. They are good people and earnest followers of Jesus.

But at the end of the day we thought our Christian life would be more than this—somehow larger, more significant, more vivid, more glorious. But it's not. Driving to church on Sunday feels a bit like *Groundhog Day,* the movie where Bill Murray's character is forced to pathetically relive exactly the same day over and over again.

There is nothing wrong with the day we Christians are reliving; it's just the same, mostly harmless routine of errands and pleasant exchanges. Our distracted gaze into the distance is occasionally interrupted by a nice hello, a small chore or a really happy worship song, but then our minds slip back into the muted monotony of our perfectly fine Christian day—and we feel vaguely discontent.

It had seemed like following Christ was supposed to be a bold adventure of power and beauty and singular importance, but the reality that keeps emerging appears to be something very different. And in very deep ways, it's disappointing.

I sense among many Christians today a subtle but deep discontent.

On the other hand, it doesn't feel right to complain, either. God has been so kind to us and our life is really so good. We have our own experiences of pain; but in a world of suffering, destruction, tragedy and disastrous dysfunction—we have been spared of and privileged with so much. So what if we're a little bored. Indeed, on most days, a little gratefulness, good cheer and routine busyness seem adequate to drive away the blues.

But then, with a relentlessness and increased frequency, the ennui returns. In fact, it begins to work its way into a good part of the larger congregation. Indeed, among many churches a familiar pattern begins to emerge. There is a thrilling experience of planting a new church, an engaging struggle through rapid growth, a creative proliferation of ministries meeting every conceivable need, an updating of facilities, excellence in worship music and programming, and a cycling through each of the latest improvements to ministry. And then, eventually, there comes a gathering discontent and a quiet, inner disappointment. Leaders look up and find themselves somehow stuck in the same routine of mediocre niceness that never seems to get near the radical drama, adventure, desperate passion and glorious power depicted in the Scriptures. Earnest, gifted, mature Christians— we feel like we are all dressed up with nowhere to go. We are left wading in the placid beach waves as the ship of adventure with Christ seems to head off to sea without us.

Now What?

Indeed, there comes a time in the life of every believer and of every church where a voice inside us simply asks, *Now what?*

After we have been introduced to Jesus and have found peace with God through him. After we have been following Christ and have gradually been surrendering the compartments of our life to him. After we have asked him to redeem our past, to heal our wounds, to reconcile our marriages and safeguard our children. After we have asked him to purify our thought life, to sanctify our ambitions, to soften our hearts, to comfort us in tragedy, to lead us in wisdom through confusion at work, at home, and in our hearts. After he has filled our minds with the Scriptures, and taught us his Word, his songs, his ways and his love for us.

After all of that, there is a voice that remains and simply asks, *Now what?*

This is, I believe, a voice of divine restlessness. This is a voice of sacred discontent. This is the voice of a holy yearning for more. This is the moment in which we can see that all the work that God has been doing in our lives and in the life of the church is not an end in itself; rather, the work he has been doing in us is a powerful means to a grander purpose beyond ourselves.

This is the supernatural moment when the rescued enter into their divine destiny as rescuers.

This is the critical transition—when we who have been rescued by Christ come to understand that our rescue has not been simply for ourselves but for an even more exalted purpose. Indeed our own rescue is God's plan for rescuing the world that he loves.

FOR WHAT?

For Christians the question *Now what?* finds its answer in the question *For what?*

For what purpose have we been rescued and redeemed? In order to know what is supposed to come next, we must have a clear understanding of the ultimate destination of our spiritual journey.

If we believe, for example, that our own rescue, redemption and sanctification in Christ is itself the ultimate destination, then the answer to the *Now what?* question is—well, nothing. Welcome to *Groundhog Day*.

But this doesn't seem satisfying does it?

In the same way that it seems fundamentally unsatisfying to make elaborate and exhausting preparations for a trip we never take. Or to sweat all season on the practice field but never actually get to play in the game. Or to plan a gourmet meal, gather the ingredients, select the spices, and slice and dice for a meal we never actually cook. Indeed, the idea that there is nothing beyond our personal spiritual development isn't meant to be satisfying—for our rescue is not the ultimate destination; it is the indispensable means by which God works out his plan to rescue the world.

THE LIGHT OF THE WORLD

In the Bible, Jesus is continually calling his disciples to look beyond their own meager aspirations and grasp the greatness of their calling. This is always hard for them to do, but Jesus keeps trying. In one of the New Testament's most famous passages Jesus asks the disciples to look beyond their own shrunken and mediocre ambition and embrace who God has made them to be:

You are the light of the world. A city on a hill cannot be hidden. Neither do people light a lamp and put it under a bowl. Instead they put it on its stand, and it gives light to everyone in the house. In the same way, let your light shine before men, that they may see your good deeds and praise your Father in heaven. (Matthew 5:14-16)

"You are the light of the world."

According to Jesus, we are it. *You* are it. The world is a dark and hurting place, and the Creator of the universe has one plan to bring light to it—and through Christ, we are that plan. Jesus is telling us that we have been rescued out of the darkness so that we can be the light of the world.

Look at the apostle Paul's words on this theme from 2 Corinthians:

If anyone is in Christ, he is a new creation; the old has gone, the new has come! All this is from God, who reconciled us to himself through Christ and gave us the ministry of reconciliation: that God was reconciling the world to himself in Christ, not counting men's sins against them. And he has committed to us the message of reconciliation. We are therefore Christ's ambassadors, as though God were making his appeal through us. (2 Corinthians 5:17-20)

Frankly, this seems like a lot to swallow. Truth be told, sometimes I'd really just rather have some light in my little world than be the light of the world. I'd settle for some more modest ambition, like being a pillar in the church or the talk of the town or maybe the ABC *World News* "Person of the Week." But Jesus calls us to more. God calls us to make the transition from being

those who have been rescued from the world,
to those through whom God is literally rescuing the world.

As C. S. Lewis has written in *The
Weight of Glory,* it's not that we have
too much ambition for ourselves; it's
that we don't have nearly enough.

> We have
> been rescued
> out of the darkness so
> that we can be the
> light of the
> world.

If we consider the unblushing promises
of reward and the staggering nature of the re-
wards promised in the Gospels, it would seem that our
Lord finds our desires not too strong, but too weak. We
are half-hearted creatures, fooling about with drink and sex
and ambition when infinite joy is offered us, like an igno-
rant child who wants to go on making mud pies in a slum
because he cannot imagine what is meant by the offer of a
holiday at the sea. We are far too easily pleased.

Given the grand and plain calling of Scripture to a bold, glorious struggle for rescue in the world, why do so many of us tend
to miss the larger calling and settle for so little?

I think there are basically three reasons.

Ignorance. First, many of us simply are not aware of the massive, urgent need for rescue in the world. We have been isolated
so long in our suburban Christian cul-de-sac that we tend to
imagine most people live like us. We know life has struggles, but
we figure most go about their days like we do: keeping our kids
healthy and safe, advancing in our jobs, tidying our yards, enjoy-

ing the holidays, hanging out with friends. Indeed, many Western Christians simply have no idea what an utter, desperate disaster is taking place twenty-four hours a day around our world. They have no vivid picture of what life is like for hundreds of millions of people in our world who live in crushing, spiritual darkness, humiliation and despair. They just don't realize that there are millions of people crying out every day to be rescued from aching, urgent hunger; from degrading and hopeless poverty; from the ravages of painful disease; from torture, slavery, rape and abuse. The vast abundance and isolation on the Disneyland island of the world's affluent communities means that many Western Christians miss God's great calling to a life of heroic rescue simply because they are largely oblivious to the need. They just can't imagine that there could really be any great heroic struggle that would need their help.

Despair. For some other Western Christians, however, lack of information doesn't seem to be the problem. It's not that they don't know enough; rather, they know too much. They know that our world is a rolling disaster of human suffering. They see the images on the news and the Internet. They hear stories and statistics on the radio and among their friends. Their problem is they have no idea what they could actually do about it.

Here the problem is not obliviousness but the paralysis of despair. Sure, maybe God wants to use me for a few doable errands of kindness in my neighborhood, but what could God possibly do with me to rescue a world from the massive hell of human suffering that lies beyond? Accordingly, when we read that Jesus calls us "the light of the world," we picture ourselves more as a nice night-light that will comfort the kids and keep us from stubbing our toe on the way to the bathroom than as a brilliant light saber that is heroically contending with the great evil of the world and driving out deep swathes of darkness. As a result, in a world crying out for rescue, we miss our larger calling from God and set for ourselves "appropriate" and more modest goals for serving his kingdom. We may even retreat backward into obliviousness because, after all, who can keep staring at horrible things you can't do anything about? Moreover, there is always great work that needs doing right here in our own cul-de-sac, right?

Consequently, while a world (and God) waits, groaning, for the people of God to bring hope, love, service and divine rescue, so many Western Christians miss their anointed work of truly glorious rescue because they are oblivious to the dramatic, ur-gent need, or they are paralyzed by hopeless despair.

Fear. But again I don't think this fully explains why so many of us miss the very calling for which we most deeply yearn, and why we find ourselves trapped, instead, in a cul-de-sac we don't want to be in. I sense there is a third obstacle that is deeper and more fundamental, and that simply is the problem of fear.

The world of disastrous human suffering is scary, and for very understandable reasons we are afraid. We actually know *a lot* about human suffering and need. We probably don't know enough, but who doesn't know that massive numbers of people in our world are desperately hurting? And truth be told, we actually *know* we probably could make a difference. We can't make a difference everywhere about everything. But we know there are people who really do make a significant and heroic difference in our world, and there is probably no reason why, in theory, we could not do so as well. So when we peel it down to the honest core of the issue, what many of us find is fear. We're scared—scared of lots of different things. In fact, we are scared of many things *already*—and we aren't even trying to rescue the world.

If we answer God's call to be the light of the world in the midst of great darkness and sign up to be the means by which Jesus is seeking to rescue the world—honestly, that simply feels intimidating. It sounds uncomfortable, scary, frustrating, exhausting and probably dangerous—and worst of all, it's unknown and out of our control. This is not why we went to college, bought a nice house in a good neighborhood, put seat belts on our kids and locked our doors at night. I did these things to *stay out* of the darkness, not to move toward it.

THE DILEMMA

So there it is. The heart of the dilemma. It seems we cannot rid ourselves of this primal, unquenchable yearning to make our lives matter. By divine hardwiring, we desperately want our lives to count—really, significantly count—for God's rescuing work in the world. And nothing else fills up the void. (We've tried.) On the other hand, we're really uncomfortable about where such an adventure might lead. While nodding affirmations in Jesus' direction as he beckons, we cannot get our feet to actually move. We desperately, deeply want something—but our heart faints in the attempt to get it.

Indeed, how do I actually live with bravery, love and significance? And how do I lead others in that path? We have all had moments and glimpses of our own courage. We've all been brave when we needed to be. The question is, how can we live more like that? In fact, how can we live like that so consistently that it becomes who we actually are?

What are we to do? I believe Jesus is eager to show us the way. In fact, I think Jesus is offering this generation a very fresh and powerful pathway to courage. And that surprising pathway is what we will look at next.

The Surprising Path
to Courage

ONE OF THE THINGS WISE AND GODLY PEOPLE seem to have discovered about God's pathways for transformation is that we rarely get to choose what the pathway will be. Gentle, respectful God usually gives us the opportunity to choose whether to go on the pathway or not—but we usually aren't the author, creator or inventor of the path. He is.

This makes sense, when I think about it. I probably don't know enough about where I am, where I want to go or how to get there to simply blaze my own path. In fact, that seems to be the whole idea of a pathway—it's a way to get to a new place for those who wouldn't be likely to get there on their own. A pathway is therefore a great gift. But it's a gift that is very hard to appreciate before it has actually delivered us to our destination. Indeed, life's best pathways to the most marvelous transformations almost always come as a surprise.

In sum, the untransformed can't invent their own path to transformation. It is rather the Creator who has the power to carve a path and the grace to mercifully light the way he has fashioned. Our job is to walk in it.

Life's best pathways to the most marvelous transformations almost always come as a surprise.

PATHWAY TO COURAGE

In this era I believe many Christians are yearning to walk on a pathway to courage. They yearn for liberation from small and trivial things, and to experience the passion and power of God on the more jagged edges of faith, where true glory lies. And I believe God is providing a very specific answer to that yearning and a very concrete path for getting there: God is calling his people to a pathway out of fear and triviality *through the struggle for justice* in his world.

And perhaps more surprising, it is a call to all his people. It's not a call to the handful of social justice zealots or slightly odd issue advocates in our faith community. Many churches miss out on God's transforming call by putting the handful of justice agitators in their congregation on some ministry subcommittee where they can do "their thing" without, hopefully, doing any harm. This effectively inoculates the rest of the congregation and directs everyone else right back onto their Christian cul-de-sac, where round and round they go.

Spiritually healthy and dynamic churches, on the other hand, have learned to equip the whole community of faith to do the things that matter to God. We have learned that we can't franchise evangelism to the eleven people on the "evangelism committee," or compassion to the "mercy ministries." Rather, sharing faith and caring for people are fundamental callings for the lives of all those who seek to follow Christ. Healthy churches equip all members to share their faith and to love needy people. Likewise, the work of justice is no less fundamental in Christ's call to discipleship and therefore no less fundamental for *every* Christian. In fact, Christ sternly rebuked the church leaders of his day for "neglecting" what he called "the more important matters of the law—justice, mercy and faithfulness" (Matthew 23:23). In doing so, Jesus was simply repeating the same list of things that the Old Testament said are good and required of us, namely, "to act justly and to love mercy / and to walk humbly with your God" (Micah 6:8). In both instances, the first calling on the short list is *justice*.

We should not be surprised, therefore, that God specifically uses the work of justice as the pathway for liberating us from the Christian cul-de-sac of triviality and small fears.

In other eras God has provided special pathways of rescue for his people—pathways to escape idolatry, cold-heartedness, mediocrity, joylessness and fear. For the early church it was trials of intense state persecution. For many followers of Jesus in the Middle Ages it was the struggle for reformation. Western Christians during the industrial revolution confronted brutal inequities and pathologies of rapid social change. For Christians in the late nineteenth and much of the early twentieth centuries it was the challenging opportunities of a vast new global missions movement. During the second half of the twentieth century, it was the challenge of bringing the love of Christ to the vast poverty of the developing world.

In each of these eras God provided pathways of struggle through which very common but authentic followers of Christ found rescue from the suffocating fears, corruption and mediocrity of religion—ways to live in the glorious power and goodness of the Redeemer's radical work in the world. Many Christians yearn for such a rescue today, and God is offering a very specific route to that rescue.

In Isaiah 58, God lays out a very compelling vision of what he offers those who follow him on this path:

> Your light will break forth like the dawn,
>> and your healing will quickly appear;
>> then your righteousness will go before you,
>> and the glory of the LORD will be your rear guard.
> Then you will call, and the LORD will answer;
>> you will cry for help, and he will say: Here am I. . . .
>
> The LORD will guide you always;
>> he will satisfy your needs in a sun-scorched land
>> and will strengthen your frame.
>> You will be like a well-watered garden,
>> like a spring whose waters never fail.

Your people will rebuild the ancient ruins
and will raise up the age-old foundations;
you will be called the Repairer of Broken Walls,
Restorer of Streets with Dwellings. (Isaiah 58:8-9, 11-12)

And to whom are such glories of spiritual health and significance offered? Very specifically to those who

loose the chains of injustice
and untie the cords of the yoke,
to set the oppressed free
and break every yoke. (v. 6)

Indeed, over and over in Scripture, God promises to pour out his presence and power on those who choose to follow him in his work of justice in the world. Certainly the work of justice brings marvelous rescue and joy to the *victims* of injustice, but God wants his people to know that the work of justice benefits *the people who do it* as well. It is a means of rescue not only for the power*less* but also for the power*ful* who otherwise waste away in a world of triviality and fear.

THE NEW CALL TO DO JUSTICE

This has, of course, been God's invitation to his people in all eras, but I believe that God has specifically tailored the work of justice for Christians of this era in order to address our need to be rescued from fear. Not in 150 years has God seemed to place before the Western church such a transforming call to justice.

Indeed, traces of God's wooing call to engage the struggle for justice seem to be emerging from a vast and diverse array of prophetic Christian voices in this era—from John Stott to Rick Warren to Pope Benedict to Bono.

God promises to pour out his presence and power on those who choose to follow him in his work of justice in the world.

Even a famous football coach who has called millions of American Christian men to a life of Christian discipleship believes it is the call to justice that promises to bring authentic life and power to the American church. Using analogies from football, Bill McCartney, in his book *Blind Spots,* writes about the way the church has become weak from playing defense all the time, that is, just trying to live lives of personal piety and righteousness. The church needs a good offense, says Coach McCartney. "By offense, I mean doing justice in the way the Bible mandates." He continues:

I believe that if we could more effectively teach justice and bring it out of our people, we would significantly upgrade our offense—and by doing so we would win the lost in far greater numbers. If we in the church really did justice today, we would turn our culture upside down for Jesus Christ. We need the high-powered offense of justice to make headway in a world deeply suspicious of religious phonies.

Doing justice, without sacrificing righteousness, is a potent way to bring life to a congregation that seems largely comatose. Doing justice, without sacrificing righteousness, is an effective way to keep our children passionate about following Jesus.

Imagine if the guys in our churches ever learned to do justice. Imagine what would happen if they got a taste of a powerful offense. I guarantee you they would come alive.

How surprising. A popular leader of a mass movement of largely suburban, socially conservative Christian men finds that the pathway out of a nearly comatose state of boredom, ineffectiveness and triviality lies in the struggle for justice. How counterintuitive. How unexpected. All of which points again to the surprising nature of God's pathways to transformation.

I have my own preferred vision for how my life ought to be transformed, but God frequently has something different and deeper in mind. As I get older and wiser, hopefully I get quicker at recognizing his path and following it. Because the truth is, we human beings can be tragically inept at fashioning a path to where we want to go.

DEATH IN THE CUL-DE-SAC

Take the cul-de-sac, for example, which is my metaphor for the world of suburban monotony and triviality that so many Western Christians find themselves trapped in. The literal cul-de-sac (i.e., a dead-end street), a feature of suburban housing developments, was designed to address homeowner anxieties about the dangers of automobile traffic in their streets. It was thought that the closed-off street would eliminate dangerous, high-speed traffic that might be especially threatening to children playing on the sidewalks and streets. Looking for a pathway to safety, human beings built cul-de-sacs. Ironically, several decades later, studies reveal that cul-de-sacs are the most dangerous residential configurations for children. It turns out that, contrary to our intuitions, children aren't injured by forward-moving traffic nearly as much as by cars backing up—which is exactly what cars do in cul-de-sacs. As a result, many cities are now seeking to ban cul-de-sac developments because of the danger for children.

Good, earnest suburban parents thought they knew a pathway to safety for their children. But they turned out to be tragically wrong. Likewise many Christians and churches in the West, seeking safety from a dangerous world, a threatening culture and personal weakness have turned inward to the prosperous cul-de-sac, only to find a spiritual atrophy, mediocrity and boredom that is lethal to the soul. But thankfully, Jesus is beckoning us to a better way. Not through the path that many of us would have expected but by means of a path laid out in Scripture thousands of years ago and well worn by a great company of Christian pilgrims from other eras. It is the route to rescue from the very specific perils of fear and pettiness that threaten this present generation, and it is the path to life for hundreds of millions of people who are suffering in our world.

It is God's call to

> seek justice,
>> rescue the oppressed,
> defend the orphan,
>> plead for the widow. (Isaiah 1:17 NRSV)

This is our call to seize today.

THE STRUGGLE FOR JUSTICE

Because the path is new to many of us, however, a number of preliminary questions need to be addressed about this struggle for justice. First, what exactly is it?

In law school they taught us that certain laws could be declared "void for vagueness." This is the eminently reasonable idea that a citizen cannot be expected to obey laws that are too vague to understand. In other words, a legal requirement can be rendered void if "persons of common intelligence must necessarily guess at its meaning and differ as to its application." Accordingly, if I got hauled into traffic court for having violated the road sign that said "Drive Appropriately," I might argue that the posted regulation was simply too vague to be fairly enforced. Even if I wanted to obey the sign, I couldn't understand what it is specifically asking me to do.

Likewise, sometimes the biblical call to justice feels like it should be declared "void for vagueness." Even if I want to obey the command of God to "do justice," it seems too hard to figure out exactly what that means. It probably means I should try to be fair and decent to people, but that isn't a very profound or helpful exhortation. It certainly doesn't feel very helpful in navigating what God calls me to in a world swirling with massive unfairness—big and small—on every side. Moreover, every kind of complicated social, economic and political problem in the world seems to make contradictory claims to "justice." It's exciting to think that God is yearning to rescue me from triviality and fear by making me part of his powerful struggle for justice in the world, but then it is immediately discouraging when I can't picture what that means or how I could actually do it.

Well, Jesus is eager to rescue us from this confusion through the clarity of his Word. The biblical teaching on justice is rich and complex, but it also provides more than enough practical clarity to get us moving forward now. One of the ways that the Scriptures help give us practical clarity is by focusing on the very specific sin of *injustice*. In other words, it might be overwhelming to try to carve out a universally satisfying definition of the "perfect marriage," but we all pretty well understand what adultery is. In a similar way, while we might get paralyzed drafting the perfect definition of *justice* that applies in all situations to all people, we can be quite clear about the very specific sin of injustice and what our response ought to be.

The sin of injustice is defined in the Bible as the abuse of power—abusing power by taking from others the good things that God intended for them, namely, their life, liberty, dignity, or the fruits of their love or their labor. In other words, when a stronger person abuses his or her power by taking from a weaker person what God alone has given the weaker person—God judges this as sin. And what has God alone given to all of his children? God has given life, liberty, dignity, and the increase that flows from a person's love and labor. Accordingly, when more powerful persons abuse their power by stealing those good things, they commit the sin of injustice.

In biblical stories this is the sin that was committed when

- Cain stole Abel's life through murder
- the Egyptians stole the Hebrews' liberty, dignity and well-being through forced slavery
- King David stole Uriah's wife and then Uriah's life
- Amnon stole Tamar's dignity, well-being and personal wholeness by raping her
- King Herod stole the lives of all the boys of Bethlehem two years and younger, ordering them killed to eliminate the newborn "king of the Jews"
- the religious leaders in Jerusalem stole the lives of Stephen and other believers through the abuse of their civil-religious power

In each of these stories (and hundreds of others in Scripture), someone who is weaker is being abused by someone who is stronger—and the weaker person is deprived of the good gifts that God has bestowed. This is why the Bible says, "Those who oppress the poor insult their Maker" (Proverbs 14:31 NRSV). Notice that in each of these stories the weaker person isn't suffering because of a random unfairness, an uncontrollable act of nature or a patch of bad luck. Rather, the weaker person is suffering because of the very intentional abuse and oppression of a stronger person. This is *injustice*—and God intends that the nature of this specific sin should be very clear to us.

And what should be our response to such injustice? Very specifically, God calls us to love those who suffer such injustice—which in the teachings of Jesus means to do for them what we would want done for us if we were being abused. Hebrews 13:3 makes it very plain when it says, "remember those who are in prison, as though you were in prison with them; those who are being tortured, as though you yourselves were being tortured" (NRSV). The biblical response to injustice is to "seek justice, rescue the oppressed, defend the orphan, plead for the widow."

MOBILIZING THE BODY OF CHRIST

At International Justice Mission this is the very specific focus of our ministry—to help inspire and mobilize the body of Christ to love those who are suffering injustice. As you might imagine, this work can be very dangerous. In fact, my colleagues in the field have endured death threats and violent assaults. They've been brutally attacked, punched in the face, mugged at knife point, kidnapped, beaten and attacked by mobs.

Given the extraordinary dangers and risks, one might reasonably ask, What is this struggle that IJM is calling Christians to engage—and is it really worth the risks? It's a question worth asking because we are calling Christians to address a very unique and distinctive problem. We are calling the body of Christ to address the problem of *aggressive human violence.*

The poorest people in our world suffer from a lot of familiar problems. They suffer from hunger, homelessness, illiteracy and sickness. And in response, all over the world, people of goodwill bring to bear familiar forms of assistance: we bring food and shelter and education and medicine.

But at the root of much of this suffering is actually a different problem—a less familiar problem—namely, violence. Many times the widow's children are hungry because bullies have stolen her land and she can no longer grow her own food. The street child is homeless because sexual abuse in the home has forced her onto the streets. The young boy is illiterate because he is held as a slave in a brick factory and can't go to school. The teenage girl has AIDS because she has been forcibly infected with the disease while held captive in a brothel.

In such cases we can't meet the root cause of suffering with the familiar remedies of food, shelter, schools or medicine. It simply doesn't meet the need. In fact, we can give all manner of goods and services to the poor, but if we do not restrain the hands of the bullies from taking it away, we will be disappointed in the long-term outcome of our efforts. As the rock-star activist Bono has learned from his work with the poor in Africa, caring for the poor is "not a matter of charity; it's a matter of justice."

This then is one of the things that makes IJM's calling to the church so different. We are calling Christians to address the distinctive problem of violence that lies *beneath* so much of the suffering of the poor—the suffering that tenaciously keeps so many of the poor in poverty.

To be clear, among the global poor, hunger, homelessness, education and medical care are massive needs worthy of our urgent attention. But the traditional remedies for these problems simply don't address the underlying problems of aggressive violence.

Violence is just different. Violence is intentional. Violence is scary. And violence causes deep scars. Accordingly, to deal with violence, Christians must be different.

> We are calling Christians to address the distinctive problem of violence that lies *beneath* so much of the suffering of the poor.

Over all these years, perhaps the most important thing I have learned about violence is that it can be stopped. But to make it stop, we have to do things differently. Let me try to explain what I mean.

Why Violence Is Different

To address any problem, we have to understand it first. And to do so, Christians can't run away from violence—Christians have to run *to* it. And when we get up close to it, we can see why it is so different from the other problems that confront the poor.

The first thing to notice is that violence is intentional. For example, one of the most brutal forms of violence affecting millions of poor women and girls in our world is sex trafficking. Lured away from their villages with promises of a good job in another city or country, millions of women and girls are abducted into forced prostitution and compelled to endure an endless nightmare of sexual assault inside the backrooms of brothels and bars.

Rather than look away from such ugliness, Christians have to actually go looking for it.

At IJM, that is exactly what we do. Almost every night, somewhere in the world, IJM undercover investigators are infiltrating the dark, violent underworld of sex trafficking to find the women and children who have disappeared into the blackness. These women and girls suffer alone, out of sight and out of mind—so someone has to go find them. It's different, but that is exactly what my IJM colleagues do.

And when we find the victims, we find they are not suffering by accident. They aren't suffering because of bad luck or a bad storm or a bad harvest or a bad bacteria. They are suffering because violent people want them to suffer. Violence is intentional.

Perhaps most intentional are sex predators visiting the developing world—like the sex tourists and pedophiles that IJM has uncovered brutalizing children in Cambodia. They traveled thousands of miles to one of the poorest countries in the world in order to open and patronize sex trafficking operations that violate the poorest and most vulnerable children. They thought about it. They planned. They very much intend to hurt their victims—and they think they will get away with it because their victims are poor. This is a different kind of problem; it requires a different approach.

Violence is also different from other problems affecting the poor because it's scary.

Unlike hunger or homelessness or illiteracy, if you try to attack the problem, it will attack you. Violence fights back.

One of the places we have seen this most starkly is in IJM's fight against slavery. As hard as it is to believe, there are millions of people in the developing world who live and die as slaves. Not as metaphorical slaves, but as actual slaves—about twenty-five million, experts say. My colleagues and I have met thousands of them.

Some are as young as a little four-year-old girl named Devi. Devi labored as a slave in a rice mill in South Asia. My IJM colleagues bravely infiltrated the hidden slave operation and rescued her and more than thirty other slaves forced by sheer terror to toil seven days a week inside the concrete walls of the rice mill. Devi's emancipation document from the government certifies that she was "forced to work under physical threat to her life."

Of course, Devi didn't become a slave accidentally or by bad luck. The slave owners planned and conspired to hold her and her family as slaves through the power of violence. Moreover, as we have learned, these men of violence fight back. In fact, in leading raids to rescue slaves, my IJM colleagues have found themselves attacked by mobs whipped up by the slave owners. They have had their vehicles smashed with bricks and rocks, and have only narrowly escaped with their lives. Recently, two of our undercover investigators seeking the release of slaves from another rice mill were captured by the owner and his thugs. Jivaj and Peter were beaten, kicked and assaulted as the thugs sought to throw them on the train tracks. By God's grace and the intervention of additional IJM operatives, Jivaj and Peter escaped without serious injury. By nature, violence fights back. This makes the problem scary—which leaves so many of the poor facing the problem utterly alone.

Finally, the problem of violence is different because it leaves such deep scars. Even after the visible wounds have healed, the violation, betrayal and humiliation often remain. These invisible scars of violence are usually hard for you and me to see. On the other hand, if you have ever had your head held under pool water to the cheers of others and felt the utter humiliation of desperately struggling for a simple gasp of air, then you know what I am talking about. You may emerge from the water with no marks or wounds that are visible, but from then on, the smell of chlorine may humble you forever.

These unique scars of violence—betrayal, humiliation, shame—make this problem different. And it demonstrates why it's not enough to treat the symptoms after the fact. We must stop violence before it attacks. And here is the good news: we can. Violence is intentional and scary, and it leaves deep scars, but it also can be stopped. We have seen it with our own eyes.

SECRETS OF VIOLENCE

After ten years of confronting violence among the poor we've learned some secrets. The vast majority of violence oppressing the poor is not driven by the overwhelming power of the perpetrators—it's driven by the utter vulnerability of the victims. Give the poor a strong, consistent advocate who won't go away, and the oppressors will simply leave them alone.

Why is that?

Well, here is the *first secret:* Those who prey upon the poor are not brave. They only prey upon the poor when they think they can. The reason these men fly all the way to Cambodia to abuse children is because they think no one will try to stop them.

> Violence is intentional and scary, and it leaves deep scars, but it also can be stopped.

In response, IJM is working with other Christians and local authorities to give vulnerable children in Cambodia and many other nations strong advocates. Working in a dozen countries, IJM finds the predators, and we don't go away until they are in jail— which is where an increasing number of them now are, either serving sentences or awaiting prosecution. In either case, they are not hurting poor and vulnerable Cambodian children any more. Even more powerfully, IJM has been training the Cambodia authorities to conduct these operations on their own—and now they do. And together, we are helping take down the welcome sign that once hung over Cambodia for foreign sex tourists and pedophiles. In doing so, Christians are simply changing the fear equation. The predators have more to fear now, and the children have less to fear—and as a result the children of Cambodia are safer today.

This then is the *second secret* we've learned over the years: Most fundamentally the predators are afraid of the truth. If you think about it, why do the violent oppressors of the poor lie about what they are doing? They do so because they are afraid—afraid that when people of goodwill hear about what the predators are doing, something bad will happen to them. And they're right— they should be afraid.

A particularly brutal set of slave owners we recently encountered in South Asia held more than twenty slaves in a rice mill. They and their thugs beat the slaves, sexually assaulted the women, even doused one slave's arm in kerosene and set it afire as punishment. They were the ones who mobilized the attack on our investigators Peter and Jivaj. But at the end of the day, a simple word of truth from Sandana—a twelve-year-old slave girl— brought down these monsters, and the slaves were released.

The story unfolded this way. After IJM secured the safety of its investigators, we were able to mobilize a police raid on the rice mill and get the slaves before a magistrate to tell their story. But as these terrorized slaves stood before the magistrate, they were too afraid to tell the truth. Their owners had forced the slaves into silence about what was happening to them and threatened to kill them if they tried to escape. One by one, the defeated slaves denied that they were being forced to work or being abused. Bit by bit, my IJM colleagues watched helplessly as the black cloud of lies descended over the proceeding and began rolling the slaves back into the abyss.

That is, until little Sandana found the courage to do what the bullies most feared: she spoke the truth.

To her parents' horror, Sandana explained that her daddy *couldn't* tell the truth, that the owner beat her daddy and that they were all afraid to say what was really happening. Struck by the raw power of innocent truth, the magistrate said he thought a child would not lie about such things. Emboldened, Sandana's father and the other slaves now confirmed the story one by one—in fact, they explained that there were still other slaves held at the rice mill who were hidden away during the raid. Immediately, the magistrate ordered official emancipation proceedings for the slaves standing before him and sent a second police detachment that secured the release of the remaining slaves. Because of Sandana's simple testimony, all of these former slaves are now free, the children are in school, and their families are now building independent lives under IJM's long-term rehabilitation program. And the slave owners are now facing just what they feared: the dogged pursuit of IJM's attorneys and the justice of the Indian authorities.

When held in slavery, Sandana and the millions of other slaves in our world do not need someone to bring them food or shelter or medicine or microloans. Right now, they need something different. They need freedom. This is the new thing Christians must bring. And as we do, we make it possible for education and economic rehabilitation to follow.

Moreover, it makes the predators decide between quitting the abuse or going to jail. And this is the *final secret* we have discovered: the oppressors of the poor are afraid of going to jail. We have found that when people go to jail for a crime they previously got away with, it changes their behavior. Now *they* are increasingly fearful.

And when the bullies fear justice, they leave poor people alone.

We have seen it happen. It takes a steady commitment over many years, but in northern Thailand, after working for six years to rescue kids and to send sex traffickers to jail, we have seen the victimization of children in the sex trade reduced by more than 90 percent in three targeted cities. That's good news for the girls whom we have been able to rescue—but it is even better news for the thousands of other children who will never have to face what those victims feared.

Moreover, our clients experience the miracle of transformation and justice that the men of violence hope we never see. They don't want us to see it because they fear the hope derived from it. They fear the truth. If you had an opportunity to meet our clients, you would see the transforming power of justice.

The problem of violence for the poor is different—and it requires a different approach by the body of Christ. At IJM, we certainly don't have it all figured out, but we are learning some things—a lot of it the hard way. And we have learned that the violence can stop. For the vulnerable poor, it must stop.

It simply requires a different approach and a different kind of courage. Jesus taught that "perfect love casts out all fear"—and I have seen this actualized in my IJM colleagues in the field.

Reflecting on the assault by the slave owners, our investigator Jivaj said this:

> I was terrified. But I thought, if this can happen to a man like me, what happens to the people in the rice mill every day? They are slapped and abused every day. When it happened to me, now I could feel it, I could feel the pain they must have every day. I want to help them even more. You can see their lives changed. When you see people changed, that is why I am not afraid to do what I do, even though I know the risks.

"Even though I know the risks." Perfect love casts out fear.

The problem of violence is different and requires a different kind of approach. A Baptist preacher named Martin Luther King Jr., who knew a lot about the problem of violence, said, "The moral arc of the universe is long, but it bends toward justice."

Dr. King had a vision of the God of justice, and he drew out courage from Christian people. Fundamentally, the struggle for justice forms a different kind of Christian—a Christian who has the steadiness of heart to look at the problem of violence and to actually do something about it. Give me a Christian who has walked with Jesus in the struggle against aggressive, violent injustice, and I will show you a Christian who has been changed by the journey.

Indeed, the struggle for justice is a unique and special pathway of transformation for Western Christians in this era. First, I believe there is no other category of Christian calling in which there is such an enormous disparity between the need in the world and the actual ministry addressing the need. Despite the hundreds of millions of people in the world who suffer violent abuse in their communities, the scale of hands-on Christian ministry addressing those needs is miniscule. While the number of people suffering from injustice is similar to the number of people suffering because of hunger, homelessness, sickness or a lack of access to the gospel, there are literally a hundred times more people and resources devoted to the latter than to the former. Certainly none of these needs is being addressed adequately, but for every dollar the Christian community spends on addressing injustice, it spends about a hundred dollars on traditional programs of poverty alleviation, compassion ministry, evangelism and discipleship. Again, it certainly is not the case that we are spending too much energy or resources on these more familiar needs—we are not. Rather, given the magnitude of the need and the urgency of the biblical mandate to "seek justice and rescue the oppressed," there is no justification for the gaping disparity in ministry resources to meet the need.

In response, I believe God is moving his church into the struggle for justice around the world, and for those who follow him, there will be transformation. The struggle for justice is special because it is not only the most neglected category of global ministry of the last hundred years but it also requires the very thing we most yearn for in our era: courage. Accordingly, nothing offers greater potential for rescuing us from our prison of triviality and small fears like the heroic struggle against oppressive violence in the world.

Moreover, nothing presents a more compelling and authentic witness of Christian faith in this era than the struggle for justice. In my experience, the courage to confront violence cannot be faked. You either show up or you do not. As the apostle James writes: "I will show you my faith by what I *do*" (James 2:18, emphasis mine). Few things are harder to do than to confront the violent forces of injustice the way Jesus taught—with love and faith, perseverance and strength, hope and humility. This is the authentic transformation that earns a hearing from a tired, suspicious and wounded world: a band of believers who move out from behind "doors locked for fear" (John 20:19) and proceed by courageous love to become "these people who have been turning the world upside down" (Acts 17:6 NRSV).

The God of Justice

I'VE NEVER TRIED TO TEACH MATH to a classroom of six-year-olds, but having raised four six-year-olds of my own, I think I know how I would do it. I would begin each day by distributing a delicious snack to all my little cherubs—unevenly. Then I would retire to my desk, take a seat and simply wait. Wait, that is, for the math to begin. And begin it will. Faster than you can say Pythagoras, my six-year-olds who got less than the others will produce a perfect mathematical proof of the injustice that has been rendered. In turn, the mathematical equation will be passionately examined and challenged by the members of the class who got more of the snack, and then they will be vigorously rebutted by the ones who got less. Eventually, it will all be presented to me in a raucous oral report at my desk. All in well under three minutes. I would use M&M's to teach whole numbers, pizza to teach geometry, Coke to teach liquid volume and red licorice ropes to teach units of measurement. Of course, I wouldn't need to do any of the instruction myself; rather, my six-year-olds would be zealously educating one another as I simply harness their innate passion for justice to draw out increasingly sophisticated powers of calculation and comparison.

As any parent of small children will tell you, children have an amazingly acute sense of justice. Even the most fractional disparity in the distribution of the most trivial family good will be met with cries of "That's not fair!" Of course, over time, parents will also note among children a powerful capacity to conveniently bend notions of justice to self-interest. A six-year-old's passion for justice is clearly not disinterested. In the hands of clever human beings, justice becomes an amazingly flexible concept. In fact, as we get older, it comes to look more like a powerful tool for getting what one wants. As a result, we adults respond with a healthy dose of suspicion to zealots who bandy about slogans of justice. Indeed, every leader of mass murder in the twentieth century (whether Hitler, Stalin, Mao, Pol Pot or the Rwandan génocidaires) painted the cry for justice over their grotesque crimes.

How confusing, therefore, for those of us in the twenty-first century who sense God's calling into a struggle for justice. Given the manipulations of humans, we find ourselves locked into a paralysis of equivocation and sophistication about this call to "seek justice." As Christians, how can we think clearly about the struggle for justice in a way that empowers us for right, responsible and effective *action* in the world—actions that are pleasing to our Maker and meaningful to those who are hurting?

GOD WANTS INJUSTICE TO STOP

Fortunately, God gives us strikingly clear teaching about the struggle for justice in Scripture. In my experience there is more than enough clarity in the Bible about how I am to respond to those who are suffering from abuse and oppression. Indeed, when it comes to biblical teaching on justice, the problem for me is not ambiguity; rather, the challenge is the Bible's bracing clarity. When it comes to injustice (i.e., the abuse of power by taking from others what God has given them), God's position is straightforward. God hates it and wants it to stop. That's what the Bible teaches.

Why does God want it to stop? Why does he hate it with such passion? Because he loves the victims of injustice so very much. God is intensely, personally present in their suffering. Indeed, he simply cannot sit still.

"Because of the oppression of the weak

and the groaning of the needy,

I will now arise," says the LORD.

"I will protect them from those who malign them."

(Psalm 12:5)

What does it mean to say that God is a God of justice?

First, God is a God of compassion. The word *compassion* comes from two Latin words that mean "to suffer with." Psalm 116:5 says, "Our God is full of compassion." He is with the victims of injustice and feels their suffering.

He is not only a God of compassion, he is also a God of *wrath*.

But what does this really mean? It means that we have a God of moral clarity. God does not respond to injustice or abuse with mild interest. He responds with vigor, with wrath, with judgment. Time and again in Scripture God promises punishment and accountability to those who perpetrate injustice. He is the God of great, righteous anger when it comes to the victims of abuse. And, frankly, when children are raped, when innocent people are murdered, I am glad to know that God responds with righteous anger. It wouldn't make sense to me if outrageous violence against the vulnerable in our world did not make God angry. It is a great relief to know that God does not sit passively or without feeling in the face of injustice in the world. Of course, God's anger is not the same as human anger—anger that is often disproportionate or of mixed motives. When God is angered, he is righteously angered.

God desires to shine light into the dark places of injustice, and he does that through us.

Finally, God is also a God of *rescue*. Psalm 10 highlights this aspect of God's character:

> O LORD, you will hear the desire of the meek;
>   you will strengthen their heart, you will incline your ear
> to do justice for the orphan and the oppressed,
>   so that those from earth may strike terror no more.
> (vv. 17-18 NRSV)

This is the God of rescue at work. He isn't just angry about injustice (the God of wrath). He isn't just sad about injustice (the God of compassion). He is also the God who rescues.

Psalm 35:10 puts it this way:

> O LORD, who is like you?
> You deliver the weak
> > from those too strong for them,
> > the weak and needy from those who despoil them.

(NRSV)

You may say, "Well, that's great that God wants to rescue the oppressed. But what is his actual plan for doing it?" Again, the answer to this question is clear in God's Word, and yet the answer is also surprising. It turns out that *we* are the plan. Speaking through the prophet Isaiah, God calls his people to

> seek justice,
> > rescue the oppressed,
> defend the orphan,
> > plead for the widow. (Isaiah 1:17 NRSV)

God desires to shine light into the dark places of injustice, and he does that through us. For those who take the Bible seriously there can be no doubt that God has given to us the work of justice in the world. Justice is not optional for Christians. It is central to God's heart and thus critical to our relationship with God.

Just Worship

WHEN I'M IN AIRPORTS, I OFTEN THINK about how important it is to get on the right plane. I don't mean a plane of a certain size, range, speed or maximum altitude, but a plane that's pointed in the right direction. If I'm on a plane that's pointed in the wrong direction, no matter how impressive its specifications, the longer and faster I am flying, the worse off I am. When two planes, one headed to Seattle and one headed to San Diego, start out at my airport in Washington, D.C., they both seem to be pointed in the same direction: west. In fact, the nose cone of one plane is pointed in a direction that is only a few inches different from the other. But after a few hours of flying, those planes can be a thousand miles apart.

Even though I've been a Christian a long time, I've increasingly realized that it doesn't matter how long I've been on my Christian journey, and it doesn't matter how fast or how high I've been flying. If I'm not headed in the right direction, I'm probably far away from what really matters to God.

"Heading in the wrong direction" was the problem with the religious leaders of Jesus' day. They had been leaders for a long time, but they were far away from what really mattered to God. That's why I'm so grateful that God gives us his Word. The Bible is a guide to understanding what matters to God. It is intended to keep us from drifting off course.

JUSTICE AND WORSHIP

The Bible gives us very clear markers of what is pleasing and displeasing to God to ensure that our lives stay on course. We know that the Bible has guideposts that show we are traveling in the right direction—an explanation of how much God loves justice. But the Bible also has other guideposts, which alert us that we are traveling in the wrong direction, toward the things that God hates. And it's worth noting how clearly God hates worship without justice. Through the prophet Isaiah he says:

> Day after day they seek me
>   and delight to know my ways,
> as if they were a nation that practiced righteousness
>   and did not forsake the ordinance of their God;
> they ask of me righteous judgments,
>   they delight to draw near to God.
> "Why do we fast but you do not see?
>   Why humble ourselves, but you do not notice?"
> Look, you serve your own interest on your fast day,
>   and oppress all your workers. (Isaiah 58:2-3 NRSV)

God answers this rhetorical question:

> Is not this the fast that I choose:
>> to loose the bonds of injustice,
>> to undo the thongs of the yoke,
> to let the oppressed go free,
>> and to break every yoke? (Isaiah 58:6 NRSV)

The Israelites were having festivals, observing fasts and praying, yet something was obviously wrong. So they asked God, "Why aren't you listening? Why aren't you paying attention?" He says to them, "Is not this what I require of you, to do justice and to release the oppressed?" God is displeased with worship that does not include the ministry of justice.

We see this also in Amos:

> For I know how many are your transgressions,
>> and how great are your sins—
> you who afflict the righteous, who take a bribe,
>> and push aside the needy in the gate. (Amos 5:12 NRSV)

Furthermore:

> I hate, I despise your festivals,
>> and I take no delight in your solemn assemblies.
> Even though you offer me your burnt offerings
>> and grain offerings,
>> I will not accept them;
> and the offerings of well-being of your fatted animals
>> I will not look upon.

Take away from me the noise of your songs;
    I will not listen to the melody of your harps.
But let justice roll down like waters,
    and righteousness like an ever-flowing stream.
(Amos 5:21-24 NRSV)

If there is no justice, God says, the songs, the assemblies and the worship are all displeasing. In fact, *displeasing* is not even a strong enough word in Isaiah 59:16—this passage describes God as being *appalled*. No other Scripture describes God as being appalled. What appalls him? Isaiah says:

> **God is displeased with worship that does not include the ministry of justice.**

Truth is lacking,
    and whoever turns from evil is despoiled.

The LORD saw it, and it displeased him
    that there was no justice.
He saw that there was no one,
    and was appalled that there was no one to intervene.
(Isaiah 59:15-16 NRSV)

God is not only displeased with injustice, he is appalled that his people are not showing up to stop it.

Why does God hate worship without justice so much? The book of 1 John explains that we cannot love God unless we love our neighbor. In 1 Corinthians 13, Paul also explains that, for all the grand and noble things we might do, if they are done without love, they are nothing more than irritating noise to God.

We don't want to be irritating to God. Instead, we earnestly desire to please him. To do so we need to rediscover some of Jesus' most basic teaching about what it means to please him.

Loving God
and Our Neighbor

A LAWYER CAME TO JESUS TO ASK HIM an important question. "Teacher," he said, "what must I do to inherit eternal life?" Jesus answered him with another question: "What is written in the Law? . . . How do you read it?" The lawyer answered, " 'Love the Lord your God with all your heart and with all your soul and with all your strength and with all your mind'; and, 'Love your neighbor as yourself' " (Luke 10:25-27).

Simple enough, right? Not if you're a lawyer. As a lawyer myself, I understand the way lawyers can complicate things to avoid obligations. The lawyer in Luke has a follow-up question: "And who is my neighbor?" Jesus then makes it clear, through the parable of the good Samaritan, that anyone in need is our neighbor.

WHAT MATTERS TO JESUS

When examining stories like this, it's always interesting to ask,

What is the question that matters to us? as compared to, What's the question that matters to Jesus? The question that mattered to the lawyer was, "Who *is* my neighbor?" The question that mattered to Jesus was, "Are you *loving* your neighbor?"

Jesus' conversation with this lawyer makes it clear that we can't love God without loving our neighbors. This has profound consequences for those who are ministry leaders. We can't lead others in loving God if we are not leading them in loving their neighbors. This point may seem obvious and hard to miss, but many religious leaders have done so over the centuries. "Anyone who does not love his brother, whom he has seen, cannot love God, whom he has not seen," wrote the apostle John. "And he has given us this command: Whoever loves God must also love his brother" (1 John 4:20-21).

> We can't lead others in loving God if we are not leading them in loving their neighbors.

But how do we actually love our neighbor? Jesus made this very simple. "Do to others what you would have them do to you" (Matthew 7:12). To love our neighbor is simply to consider how we would want to be treated—and then treat all others that way.

What does this have to do with understanding God's passion for justice? Simply this: doing justice is being obedient to Jesus' command to love our neighbor in a world of injustice. Doing the work of justice is practicing the one command that sums up all of the Scriptures: To love God with our heart, soul and mind, and to love our neighbor as ourselves. Justice is doing for others what we would want done for us. This is why Hebrews 13:3 puts the work of justice in the context of love, exhorting us to "remember those who are in prison, as though you were in prison with them; those who are being tortured, as though you yourselves were being tortured" (NRSV).

For those neighbors around the world who are suffering injustice, we can't say that we love them if we do not draw near and seek justice on their behalf. We must seek to rescue our neighbors with the dedication and urgency with which we would go about trying to rescue our own family or even ourself. In a world of injustice, loving intervention on behalf of the oppressed is simple obedience to Jesus' most fundamental command to love our neighbor.

For those who take the teachings of the Bible seriously, there can be no doubt that the call to seek justice is fundamental to our devotional life as Christians. The weight of the biblical material is overwhelming. This massive biblical mandate has been marginalized in most of our churches over the last hundred years, but God is calling his people back to these neglected fundamentals. Our job is to respond to the calling when we hear it—for it is God's grace to us.

OUR HOPE FOR JUSTICE

Unfortunately, it seems that the global media hold more weight than the biblical material when it comes to our understanding of injustice. Television portrays the struggle for justice as a hopelessly lost cause. Most days, the weight of triumphant evil and violence in our world feels utterly crushing. I think many Christians would avail themselves of the courage God offers if they thought there was a chance that it would actually do any good. But given the dark headlines that assault us day after day, defeating injustice doesn't seem very plausible. In fact, it feels rather naive or immodest to imagine that we could actually make a difference in the face of massive, aggressive evil and violence in the world.

While these discouraging musings are certainly understandable, we should know that they are utterly unimportant to God. First, such notions of hopelessness say to God: You are a God who calls your people to ministry without providing any power to actually do it. If that is what we honestly believe, we should just clearly say so. Though the Bible doesn't say this about God's character, it's okay for us to say it. Acknowledging that we are struggling with what the Bible teaches about the character of God is often the first, best step to authentic faith. Indeed, as Dallas Willard points out in *Renovation of the Heart*, we don't believe something by merely *saying* we believe it, or even when we *believe* that we believe it. We believe something when we *act* as if it were true.

When it comes to praying and working for justice, Jesus could hardly have been more explicit about our perseverance in faith:

Then Jesus told them a parable about their need to pray always and not to lose heart. He said, "In a certain city there was a judge who neither feared God nor had respect for people. In that city there was a widow who kept coming to him and saying, 'Grant me justice against my opponent.' For a while he refused; but later he said to himself, 'Though I have no fear of God and no respect for anyone, yet because this widow keeps bothering me, I will grant her justice, so that she may not wear me out by continually coming.'" And the Lord said, "Listen to what the unjust judge says. And will not God grant justice to his chosen ones who cry to him day and night? Will he delay long in helping them? I tell you, he will quickly grant justice to them. And yet, when the Son of Man comes, will he find faith on earth?" (Luke 18:1-8 NRSV)

While the Bible does not teach that we will prevail in every battle against injustice on this earth, it does teach us that God will prevail in the ultimate war, that he goes with us into every battle, that he brings his power and protection to bear on our behalf, and that he will prevail in all battles necessary to the ultimate triumph of his kingdom. In a world of groaning injustice, these are the truths that Jesus invites his followers to believe—and act on.

I don't know if Jesus actually rolls his eyes, but that is what I picture him doing every time he hears the "realistic" and "mature" Christians give fourteen reasons why there is nothing we can do to stop violence and injustice. I think he is very sympathetic to our honest fears. But I think he is just annoyed when those fears are dressed up in a sophisticated analysis of why nothing will work. He's understandably irritated, I think, because he hears us simply regurgitating the ancient, tired nostrums of the father of lies, who for millennia has been making one simple argument, namely, that what God has plainly said about himself, the world and history isn't true. Since God can't be trusted, we, the enlightened ones, will figure out this dangerous world for ourselves.

Needless to say, Jesus is annoyed because of what this says about our heavenly Father, and also because of the way such despair becomes a self-fulfilling prophecy. It is historically accurate to say with Edmund Burke that "all that is necessary for the triumph of evil is for good men to do nothing." If people of goodwill lose all hope and simply give up in the struggle against evil, then indeed, evil will triumph. On the other hand, if people of goodwill persevere in hope, evil must eventually give way. That is why the struggle for justice always stands or falls on the battlefield of hope. And this is why the great pivot point of history occurred with Jesus Christ. As Dallas Willard reminds us, this first-century rabbi turned the worldview of the ancients upside down by teaching that hope was a virtue. Prior to Jesus, the ancient philosophers viewed hope as a weakness, a vulnerability of the naive and simple-minded. For the early followers of Jesus, however, hope distinguished those who knew God from those who did not (Ephesians 2:12; 1 Thessalonians 4:13).

For these reasons, while our arguments against the impracticality of doing justice are understandable, they are ultimately not very interesting to Jesus. Nor are they very helpful to the slave boy or to the prisoner being tortured or to the widow brutally thrown off her land. Imagine yourself enslaved in a rice mill or handcuffed on a concrete floor or violently chased from your own home, and then picture yourself listening to millions of Christians explain why there is nothing they can do to help you. Wouldn't such explanations be infuriating? Mostly because they would be, for the most part, untrue. Wouldn't you long to hear someone—anyone—speak up and say, "Wait! We may not be able to do everything, but can't we help *this* one?"

> We don't believe something by merely *saying* we believe it, or even when we *believe* that we believe it. We believe something when we *act* as if it were true. (Dallas Willard)

HARD FACTS OF HISTORY

This then is the ultimate paradox of our despair over injustice. It masquerades in the robes of hard thinking, realistic analysis and modesty, and dismisses hope as illusory, naive and even arrogant. But truth be told, it is despair that has the facts wrong. In the long run, it is always the tyrants and bullies who end up on the ash heap of history. Sometimes the moral arc of the universe is long indeed. Sometimes unbearably long. But on both small and epic scales, it does bend toward justice. And miraculously, God has given into human hands the power to bend it more quickly to its ultimate destination. This is what the facts of history tell us. Indeed, God intends that our hope in the work of justice be built not simply on bare theological assertions about the character of God but also on the hard factual evidence about the track record of God.

Hope is not simply wishful thinking; it is a fruit of the Spirit born of the spiritual discipline of remembering. This is why, even in the darkest eras, God has left us a witness of what happens when his people believe and follow him in the fight for justice. In the next chapter we will meet three people whose witness could not be more dramatic or breathtaking, and yet almost none of us have heard their stories. Here is an opportunity to remember what surprising things God can do.

Charging the Darkness

WHEN MY CHILDREN WERE VERY YOUNG, there were evenings when they were simply too afraid to go to bed.

"My room is scary," they would whisper.

"Well, why is your room scary?" I would ask.

"Because it's dark," they would reply.

Try as I may to find a specific reason for their fear, the fact of the matter was they were afraid because their room was dark. And no amount of fine, rational discourse was going to drive out the fear.

Over time, I eventually found that there was only one solution to this dilemma. They would have to actually see someone charge into the darkness of their bedroom and come out alive. Thus was born our "charge the darkness" ritual for evenings when lights-out was just too scary. Positioning the children outside the doorway to their bedroom, I would bravely offer to charge the darkness and see what would happen. Standing attentively in their footy pajamas, the children would stand back in the hallway and watch as I, with a running start, threw myself into the dark oblivion of their bedroom. Enveloped by the dreaded darkness, I would freeze in the middle of the room. My children, clutching stuffed animals, waited breathlessly outside the room, watching with me to see what great terror the dark would bring. And each time, nothing came. Not a thing. Giggling over the anticlimax, they would line up one by one to charge the darkness—finding, as I had, that the dangers of their bedroom had been vastly overrated.

What they needed was to see someone else charge the darkness *first,* and then quite marvelously they found their chains of fear melting away.

What they needed was to see someone else charge the darkness *first,* and then quite marvelously they found their chains of fear melting away.

When it comes to the struggle for justice, God has likewise sent many of his saints to charge the darkness ahead of us so we can actually see what a difference simple obedience can make. If we were more familiar with their stories, we would likewise find our shackles of doubt and fear increasingly falling away.

William, Donaldina and Irena are good examples. For those who doubt that it is possible to make a difference in a world of the most violent and brutal oppression, I offer their stories as evidence to the contrary. What makes their stories all the more delightful and powerful is the fact that not one in a hundred thousand Western Christians have ever heard their epic tales. This suggests that when it comes to assessing what is and is not possible in the struggle for justice, we don't have all the facts on the table. Indeed, after we get to know William, Donaldina and Irena, we won't be so modest in defining what God can and cannot do to bring justice through his people.

Simply put, because of the loving courage of these three believers, thousands of very vulnerable people were rescued from the most brutal and vicious oppressors of their day. In each case, they could have easily avoided any contact with the plight of those who were being abused; instead, they intentionally sought them out. They didn't work for large or powerful global institutions, they were disadvantaged in the society from which they came, and they lived happy and long lives, well after the demise of the powerful tyrants they fought.

WILLIAM SHEPPARD

At the turn of the twentieth century, perhaps the most brutal and grotesque human rights disaster on earth was taking place silently in the heart of Africa. Blaise Pascal once wrote that all the world's great suffering came from the fact that kings did not know how to sit quietly in their own rooms. Indeed, in the 1880s King Leopold of Belgium found he could not sit quietly, and as a result millions of innocent human beings were murdered and destroyed. It all began when King Leopold decided it was time for his recently created but diminutive kingdom to have a proper colony like the bigger kingdoms of his day. Looking about the globe, however, he found that these other kingdoms had already laid claim to most of the earth's land mass, and that the only thing left over was the unexplored interior of Africa. Accordingly, King Leopold raised a private army to seize what is now the Congo for his personal possession.

Obsessed with finding something of value to extract from his new colony, King Leopold found that the Congo was rich with rubber plants that might feed the burgeoning industrial revolution of his day. But there was one problem. The work of harvesting the rubber was so difficult that the local residents refused to do it. Accordingly, King Leopold unleashed his infamous private army, the Force Publique, upon the Congolese population to force them to harvest the rubber and perform other services. Over the next two decades, the campaign of forced labor destroyed about half of the population of the Congo. The Force Publique used whips, chains and brutal beatings to compel the labor. To force the men to work, the Force Publique imprisoned and raped women they held as hostages. They burned down villages and accumulated piles of severed hands and ears in their campaign of unrestrained violence and terror. As the local Belgian authority wrote home to his government: "To gather rubber in the district . . . one must cut off hands, noses and ears."

Eventually the horror and pathology would be famously described in *The Heart of Darkness* by Joseph Conrad, but for many years the nightmare took place out of sight and out of mind from the rest of the world. All of this slaughter and horror was carefully hidden from the world through an intentional, aggressive and expensive campaign of deceit and propaganda perpetrated by King Leopold and his minions. What finally brought it all out in the open was the courageous documentation of William Sheppard, an African American missionary of the Presbyterian Church from Virginia. A son of freed slaves, Sheppard had pushed past the discrimination that formally barred him within his denomination from leadership in missionary work, and he made his way to the Congo only a few years after the first Europeans had set foot in the interior of Africa.

Sharing the gospel and planting churches in the Congo, Sheppard won the trust of the indigenous people and soon found himself confronted with the grotesque horror that was being perpetrated upon the Congolese people by its Belgian rulers. Braving violence, disease, death threats and unimaginable hardship, Sheppard risked everything to work with other concerned missionaries and advocates to properly document the atrocities—including an undercover investigation of a Force Publique massacre that required Sheppard to individually count eighty-one severed hands. Sheppard's report of the massacre eventually launched the world's first international human rights campaign: the Congo reform movement. Sheppard was aggressively attacked by King Leopold in a nearly devastating and corrupt libel suit—but Sheppard was acquitted, and the campaign eventually forced an end to the atrocities in the Congo.

DONALDINA CAMERON

While William Sheppard was contending with the horrors of
King Leopold in distant Africa, back home in America during the
same era, a young missionary intern found herself doing battle
with a vast and violent business of rape for profit that brutalized
tens of thousands of women and girls in San Francisco. Born in
1869, about five years after William Sheppard, Donaldina Cam-
eron grew up in a loving Christian home on rugged ranches in
the wild west of California in the decades
following the gold rush. By the 1880s
she had enrolled in a teacher's college in Oakland but was forced
to abandon her education
when her father died.
Donaldina had hoped
to get married and raise
children on a ranch, but one
day a family missionary friend began sharing shocking stories of the il-
licit commercial sex trade operating in the
alleys and warrens of Chinatown in San Francisco. Indeed, tens
of thousands of girls were being shipped in from China and sold
as slaves to feed the appetites of the overwhelmingly male population. The youngest girls were sold as house servants and the
teenage girls were sold into prostitution, a trade so vicious that
most died within five years. The horrors were unspeakable.

> After we get
> to know William,
> Donaldina and Irena, we
> won't be so modest in
> defining what God can and
> cannot do to bring
> justice through
> his people.

Donaldina found herself seized by the plight of the Chinese girls who were being brutalized as sex slaves, and when her friend asked her if she would be willing to intern with a small Presbyterian mission outpost that was trying to rescue and restore the girls, the twenty-five-year-old Donaldina accepted the offer. Within a few months of her arrival in the dark epicenter of this brutal sex trade, the leader of the mission fell ill, and Donaldina eventually found herself managing the mission. She never left.

Over the next forty-five years Donaldina endured death threats, assaults and corrupt authorities. She rescued and restored more than three thousand girls from sex slavery through daring night-time raids in which she, along with the police, wielded ax and sledgehammer. In her lifetime Donaldina would see the end of the notorious "yellow slave trade" in her community.

Irena Sendlerona

Just as Donaldina was seeing the light of God's love and justice vanquishing the darkness of commercial rape in San Francisco, on another continent, the darkness of Nazi genocide was descending over the Jewish ghettos of Poland. In the 1940s a modest, young Catholic woman, Irena Sendlerona, was introduced to the suffering of hundreds of thousands of Jews incarcerated in the Warsaw Ghetto—a hell where four thousand Jews per month died from the brutality. While most of her Polish neighbors remained silent and avoided any contact with the ghetto, Irena used her position with the city's Social Welfare Department to secure a special permit to visit the ghetto areas for "combating contagious diseases."

Knowing full well that aiding and abetting the rescue of Jews from the ghetto was a crime punishable by death, young Irena proceeded to develop an underground network to smuggle Jewish children to safety. Eventually captured by the Gestapo, Irena was interrogated and tortured and her limbs brutally crushed. While being driven out for execution, a bribed guard knocked her unconscious and dumped her in a ditch. By God's grace, Irena survived and continued her rescue efforts, eventually rescuing over 2,500 Jewish children during the war. Irena long outlived the vicious Nazi tyrants of her day, and lives today to bear witness to the power of Christian love at the ripe old age of ninety-seven.

The next time you wonder about how God is working in the world, remember William, Donaldina and Irena.

These stories from other eras are offered to us as a powerful witness of what God can do through a single life of courage to drive out even the darkest evil and to bring tangible rescue to thousands of lives. Indeed, over the last ten years with IJM, I have seen with my own eyes what God can do in our era to win justice for thousands of people brutalized by violent forces of injustice. Anyone who thinks there is nothing we can do to overcome aggressive forces of evil in our world has not seen what my IJM colleagues and I have witnessed over the last decade. But some of the most powerful encouragement has come not from the legions of lives that have been changed, but from the few—the individual stories of dramatic, heroic transformation that God has won.

The Witness of One

WHEN IT COMES TO THE POWER OF God's love in the world, the greatest witness frequently comes in the story of the one. But it often takes some effort to draw these stories out. As part of my job I spend a lot of time with very poor people in the developing world, and to be honest, their lives are so dramatically different from my own that it can be hard to find a point of authentic human connection. They seem to live in a universe of shanties, dirty water, empty stomachs and soiled clothes, and I frankly come from a completely different solar system.

After the first few choruses of "We Are the World" have been sung, it's pretty hard for me to actually keep up a conversation with someone who—in terms of nutrition, housing, medical care and protection from abuse—literally doesn't live as well as my dog does back home. That's just honest. So what could we possibly talk about? At what common point of human experience could we actually connect?

Interestingly, over time, I have found a nearly universal point

of contact: the experience of being a parent. Parenting seems to
be the great leveling experience among human beings, especially
in the unique sense of vulnerability that mysteriously accompa-
nies parents of all places. Parents all over the world love their
kids, and yet none of us (rich or poor) can control what happens
to them.

Of course, some of us can control more things than others,
but we all have moments when we know our heart is actually
walking around in someone else's body, and we can't control
the outcome. For all parents, waves of emotions heave involun-
tarily within us when the doctor reports that the test doesn't
look good, or when our spouse says, "No, I thought she was with
you" at a crowded amusement park, or when a police officer calls
and says he's sorry but there's been an accident. In those moments it doesn't matter who you are or what you own. You have
entered into the swirling vortex of vulnerability that comes with
being a parent.

That's why, whether in a slum, a village or a barrio, when I
sit with parents, I get that sympathetic and knowing smile when
I bring out the crinkled snapshots of my little kids. Even when
we cannot exchange a single word in the same language, we can
always exchange glances that say, "Oh, you love yours too—and
you can't control the ending either, can you?"

Of course that's precisely the sympathetic smile I try to share
with all the parents on the plane when we arrive in my hometown,
Washington, D.C. Dressed in their new vacation wear and cheer-

fully juggling kids and strollers and snacks and coloring books, mom
and dad disembark for their long-anticipated and minutely planned
vacation in the nation's capital. Of course, I see these parents and
kids again when I'm leaving town and they are returning home—
exhausted beyond recognition, juggling and spilling stuffed animals
and orange juice, parents feuding and barking, children crying and
stomping, embarking together with grumpy fatigue on their all-too-
quick return to the world of fallible parenting.

Straddling that yawning chasm between the parents we'd like
to be and the parents we are, these moms and dads are, for me,
a picture of how earnestly we want to be good parents, but how
hard and humbling the experience actually is. In the end, we all
need a lot of grace. And this, I find, is universal. All around the
world, rich or poor, parents encounter their own weakness and
their deepest vulnerability in their love for their children. We
love so much and can control so little.

MARY

And here is where I have found such a mysterious and unexpected connection to people in the developing world whose lives
are otherwise so different from my own. Mary, for example, is
a Cambodian woman who lives in a different universe than me;
she lives in a squatter area in Phnom Penh. But she is also a parent. And like me, she has a daughter. But her daughter has been
missing—for weeks.

Mary and her husband struggle to put food on the table, and

some local women had offered to take Bopha, their sixteen-year-old daughter, to the port city of Koh Kong where she could reportedly get a job peeling shrimp. Mary had repeatedly refused the offers because, like most of us, she didn't want her teenage daughter to go so far away, and Mary worried what might happen to her. But one day Bopha was gone. Simply gone. Mary heard nothing for weeks, and for weeks she couldn't eat or sleep. Friends and neighbors told her that Bopha was probably dead. "I died too," Mary said.

In the end, we all need a lot of grace.

Later, Mary received shocking news. A neighbor reported that a friend had actually seen Bopha alive—but she was hundreds of miles away, across the border in Thailand, and locked in a brothel. It turns out that the people offering to take Bopha for a job peeling shrimp were actually working for sex traffickers.

These patient predators ultimately prevailed on Bopha's own sense of financial obligation to her family and convinced Bopha to go with them without telling her mom. Soon, like hundreds of thousands of other teenagers in Asia, Bopha found herself transported hundreds of miles from her home and sold into a brutal brothel where she was beaten into submission and forced to submit to repeated rapes from paying customers.

As soon as Mary heard about her daughter, she did what you and I would do—she ran to the police to get their help. But her local police just made excuses—and demanded money, which Mary didn't have. "We had no money," Mary said. "We could not do anything."

"We could not do anything."

See, I don't care who you are, where you are from or what you do or don't own; if you have ever had a child in trouble, you and Mary are now in the same universe. It's not just the child who is in trouble, but now *you're* in trouble—because your heart is walking around in somebody else's body. Your kid is in trouble—and while *you* would do *anything,* you are, by some nightmarish conspiracy of circumstances, stuck with Mary saying, "We can't do anything." That is the wrenching vulnerability of loving someone very much in an unsafe world—and I would venture to guess we all know something of such deep waters. Even if you are not a parent, if you have ever loved another person deeply in their moment of desperate peril—a sister, a friend, a nephew, a parent—you know what it is like to be helplessly dangling with them over the abyss of ruin. If any of us have ever felt the stomach-churning panic of desperate love, then it turns out that Mary is not a total stranger to us after all. Mary is not a stranger—she is a human being who loves deeply, and like all of us, she needs some help. And fortunately, it is actually possible to help mothers like Mary.

In fact, it doesn't take much prodding to get Kaign Christy, the director of IJM's office in Cambodia, to respond to such cases, because he is a parent too; in fact, he also has a teenage daughter about Bopha's age. Not only is he a sympathetic father, but he and his IJM colleagues have also been training a special Cambodian police unit to fight sex trafficking and other crimes against children in Cambodia. It's great to be a sympathetic parent, but it is even better to be a sympathetic parent with a police unit. In fact, the IJM team was able to follow investigative leads and take a police contingent across the border to rescue Bopha and to eventually rescue nine other women and children abducted by the same trafficking ring. IJM was also able to prevent the victimization of scores of additional girls by securing the arrest and conviction of the brothel keeper and five traffickers, who will spend the next decade in prison instead of selling and raping children.

What matters most to Mary, of course, is that she has her daughter back. In fact, Bopha is being cared for in one of our partner aftercare centers where she is doing well. Bopha receives treatment for her trauma and vocational training for her future.

This is what her mom told us:

> When Bopha was taken, it was very hard for me. . . . No one believed I would ever get my daughter back. IJM was my backbone, because I could not stand up to this without you. When I learned that IJM and the police had rescued her in Thailand I felt like I was born again. For days, I did not feel like I was walking on land, but floating in the heavens. . . . She is in a good place and receiving good training. I now have hope for my daughter's future.

Venus Soko

Hope for our children's future—I think that is just about all we fundamentally ask for our children. And yet what heartache it is for parents to endure the slow-motion nightmare of watching helplessly as that hope steadily slips away. Venus Soko is another one of those residents of the developing world who lives on that remote solar system somewhere past Pluto where the global poor live. She lives in the beautiful country of Zambia in Southern Africa, but hunger and disease and destitution mar the landscape of her life so thoroughly that it is hard for someone like me to relate to her. But there is one thing about Venus I can understand, and that's her love for her children. And that's precisely what makes her story so intolerable for me.

Venus has been trying to provide for her children on her own ever since disease swept her husband away. Together they had operated a couple of small stalls selling food and other items at the market, and they managed to bring home food and dignity to the children.

But now with her husband gone Venus is just another vulnerable widow in Africa who has had her property and her business stolen from her by a bully in the community. The bully has allowed her to keep nothing. For herself, she is down to a single garment, which she has worn for months. There are no more coals for the fire and no food in the pots. Now she watches with desperation each day as her son literally grows crippled from malnutrition. Like Mary, *she would do anything*—but finds she can't do anything on her own, only watch as her son's legs slowly wither and bow into uselessness. She needs some help. Like thousands of other widows in Africa, she doesn't need someone to take care of her children; she just needs help getting her property back so *she* can take care of her children.

Gratefully, Christians can bring rescue. Indeed, Colonel Clement Mudenda, the recently deceased director of our office in Zambia, was yet another sympathetic father—and this time, a sympathetic father who was also a lawyer with a court order. As he did for hundreds of other widows and orphans, our IJM director and his staff were able to restore Venus's property and help her reestablish her business. Venus's little café is now prospering. She is feeding her children and plowing profits back into the business, and can afford rudimentary therapy to help restore the strength of her son's limbs. She does not have to watch her children wither and die as she once did because of thieves in her community. IJM has placed the law on her side and has trained thousands of community leaders in Zambia to do the same for vulnerable widows and orphans in their own neighborhoods.

> As parents, it turns out we don't need much; we just need a fighting chance for our children—and that's what compassionate Christians provide to parents like Venus.

As parents, it turns out we don't need much; we just need a fighting chance for our children—and that's what compassionate

Christians provide to parents like Venus. Maybe we've all been in that scary place where a friend or a neighbor or a doctor had to come to the rescue for one of our own. And if you can remember that trembling sense of gratitude that came in waves over you when you tried to say thank you, then you know something of how Venus greets us when we visit her and her children. No one should ever have to be that grateful, but sometimes we are— because we all need help.

NAGARAJ

Nagaraj needed help. He has three little boys and he loves them. But he can't take them to the doctor when they are sick, and he can't send them to school. Not because there aren't doctors in his village or schools nearby but because Nagaraj and his children are actually owned by someone else. They are slaves. They are forced to live in concrete cells inside the four walls of a brick factory. Along with about eighty other slaves, Nagaraj and his wife work sixteen hours a day, six days per week, making and carrying bricks. If anyone tries to run away, he or she is chased down, dragged back and beaten in front of the others.

Nagaraj and his children will spend their entire lifetime as slaves in the brickyard. The children will typically start with a few bricks upon their head—maybe four bricks, weighing a total of about 25 pounds—until they work up to carrying loads of 75 to 120 pounds, making a hundred trips a day across the brickyard. All just to wake up and do it all over again.

Of course, as parents our most basic instinct is to provide for and protect our children. But for Nagaraj, and millions of slaves in our world like him, imagine the deep humiliation of knowing he can't protect his children from endless toil and abuse. These parents don't even "own" them—someone else does. And I can tell you from having spent time with Nagaraj that he isn't a different species of parent than you or I.

He doesn't get used to it. He doesn't look at his boys and see barnyard livestock created for a mindless existence under a harness. He views them as delightful children of his own.

His mind turns over and over furiously—*How can I get them to the doctor? How can I get them to school? How can I get them out of here?* But he needs help and, as we do in our most desperate moments as parents, he simply cries out to God.

And joyously, for Nagaraj and his wife and boys, God has answered his prayers. He answered his prayers by moving the heart of another sympathetic father—a father who just happens to direct IJM's antislavery work in South Asia. Blair Burns is a sympathetic father with young children about the same age as Nagaraj's. Moreover, he also has a unit of professional undercover investigators.

Our director sent those undercover agents to infiltrate the brick factory, and they successfully videotaped the slaves at work and the overseer's own explanation of how they chase down and punish the slaves that try to run away. Nagaraj bravely managed to smuggle scores of his fellow slaves out of the factory for brief rendezvous with our investigators to prepare sworn statements of their bondage. Armed with this overwhelming evidence, IJM was able to mobilize a police raid on the factory and secure the rescue of nearly eighty slaves. The slave master's factory is now shut down and he is facing prosecution.

Most importantly for Nagaraj, his children are free—free to play, free to go to school. And for Nagaraj, this is no small thing. His children are no one's possession. Their daddy is not a slave but a man. He is a provider, a protector. He is a father.

And this is all he asked God for—just a chance to be a good father, a good husband, a good man. And how happy God must be to see the results. To see what we see. The way Nagaraj loves and delights over his children. To see the way he honors his wife. To see the way they have worked together to build a brick business of their own. To see the way he leads the association of former slaves as they rebuild their lives together. To see the way he has volunteered to work with IJM to rescue other slaves.

A FIGHTING CHANCE

But he needed a little help. And I relate to that because I'm a parent—and my heart is walking around in someone else's body. And that is how I connect to parents all over the world who today are simply asking us for a chance—a chance to find their kids, a chance to feed their kids, a chance to protect their kids. They don't ask us to do these things for them. They can take care of their own families, but at the moment they need a hand so they can have a fighting chance. And I think we all want to give it to them. Because it's right. Because it's good. Because it's joy.

And that, very simply, is what God invites us to in this struggle for justice in the world. He invites us to play our part in driving out the darkness for parents like Mary, Venus and Nagaraj. To be very concrete and practical about it, I offer two appendixes at the end of the book with tangible steps you can take to begin your own journey on God's great expedition of justice. Jesus wants us to know that through us lives can be changed. And in the process God offers to change us, to grant us courage and to drive out the gathering darkness of small fears.

Seizing the Gift of Courage

DEEP WITHIN ALL OF US THERE IS A yearning to be brave. And like all of our deepest, truest and best yearnings, it comes from how we were made. Courage—the power to do the right thing even when it is scary and hard—resonates deeply with the original shape of our soul. Why this should be so, however, is not outwardly obvious. Indeed, apart from the inexplicable and indelible imprint of our Maker, it's not clear why it should matter to us that we should be brave. Why is it so beautiful to see someone do the right thing when it is hard? Why, on the other hand, should there be such shame about our cowardice? Why should it matter so much to my inner being that I do the right thing rather than the safe thing? It's a mystery. But there it is, pointing relentlessly to the nature and delight of the One who made me.

In fact, the beauty and goodness for which we were fashioned by our Maker is more glorious than we dare to imagine. When it comes to being brave, we should picture the courage of Jesus—the power to fearlessly speak the truth, the freedom to selflessly love, the strength to unflinchingly stretch oneself on a cross. And the truth is, in our deepest core we were actually made to be like *that*.

But by the tragedy of the Fall—and countless choices we have made over the many minutes and miles of our lives—we find our soul quite different from what our Maker intended. This reality is no doubt familiar to us and generally fills us with habitual despair. What is infinitely more interesting, however, is not how far we have taken ourselves from what was intended, but how powerful and unrelenting our yearning remains. Even now, in spite of all the water under the bridge, we so want to be brave. Our soul sings when properly reminded of the courage and goodness for which we were made, and we weep when we look upon our moments of failure. Hallelujah! For by this we know that the heart of our Maker lives. It still pounds within us—muffled, neglected,

Deep within all of us there is a yearning to be brave.

stifled, denied and stricken—and yet beating, wooing, yearning, weeping. Who we truly are and were meant to be is evidenced more by our yearnings than by our history.

This is the grace of God, that even now he sets before us a pathway to courage and boldness of heart. The question is, how can we prepare ourselves to receive this grace? The path is a gift we did not earn or merit, but now that it is offered to us, will we seize the opportunity to follow this unexpected pathway of grace? What steps can *we* take to prepare ourselves for the journey?

Here are three steps that my colleagues and I at the International Justice Mission have been working on to prepare ourselves to seize this grace of courage.

Do Less, Reflect and Pray More

Reflect about the life you are living, about the anxieties you are carrying and about the life you sense God is calling you to live. As I mentioned before, as busy as we are at IJM with urgent operational matters of life-and-death significance, we begin every morning by spending thirty minutes doing absolutely "nothing." For thirty minutes every day we just sit quietly, reflecting, praying and preparing spiritually for the day. Then at 11 a.m. we gather again to pray—every day.

There are, in fact, very deep roots to our fears, and we need to be quiet enough long enough to explore them. For many of us the first step in preparing ourselves for a role in rescuing others is to acknowledge and receive *our* rescue by God.

Many of us *say* that Jesus has rescued us from judgment and sin and death—but actually we are quite busy trying to save ourselves. What sometimes looks like confident hard-charging activity in the world is frequently just nervous energy generated by what terrifies us. The fear that God won't accept us without our merit badges. The fear that people won't love us if we don't get As on our projects. The fear that our life isn't significant if its worth can't be measured in the quality and quantity of our things.

Will you really be significant if you own that? If you live there? If you get that position? If you are included in that group? *Or* is your significance established because the Creator of the universe made and redeemed you?

The first step for many of us, therefore, is to truly receive our rescue from Christ. To return to that place of grace where our worth—our rock-solid worth—is affirmed fully and without condition by our Creator, our Maker, the Lover of our soul who died for us and fully redeemed us. If we have not found how profoundly God cares for us, we will not be equipped to care for the needy world that lies beyond us.

> Many of us *say* that Jesus has rescued us from judgment and sin and death—but actually we are quite busy trying to save ourselves.

Search the Promises of Scripture and Take a Risk

Take Christ at his word and see if he is true. If you're wrestling with some sort of decision, reflect for a moment and ask yourself, *Am I being brave, or am I being safe?* In the end, it depends on whether we think God can be trusted.

For many of us the fundamental question is, *In my Christian life, do I see myself playing offense or defense?* Many Christians are so busy defending their own end zone that they have forgotten the joy of scoring touchdowns. We fret over what might happen to our stuff, our reputation, our standing, our children, our ideology and our investments, and in the process we forget that we have these things so we can live fully for Christ. All the things we value were never meant to be *safeguarded.* They were meant to be *put at risk and spent,* for we are in a life-and-death battle (Ephesians 6:10-13). Thus, in one of Jesus' parables, when a servant reported that he had successfully safeguarded what the master had entrusted to him, the master's response was, "You wicked, lazy servant" (Matthew 25:26).

Moreover, in the work of building his kingdom, Jesus promises that "the gates of hell shall not prevail against it" (Matthew 16:18 KJV). In other words, God, not the forces of evil, is on the offensive. And according to Jesus, hell is decisively on the losing side. Listening to some Christians, though, we would think that hell is the aggressor and that we need to defend ourselves. But of course, gates are never on the offensive. Gates don't move out— they keep out.

Using another metaphor, Jesus says the forces of darkness cannot resist the forces of light. That of course is the nature of light—when it encounters darkness, light wins every time. Picture a pitch-dark room with no windows and only a single door, which is shut. Outside the door is a brightly lit hallway. When the door is opened, will the darkness snuff out the light or vice versa? Of course, the light prevails. Indeed, "This is the message we have heard from him and declare to you: God is light; in him there is no darkness at all" (1 John 1:5).

Who has been overcome by darkness and is having a hard time believing that God is good? Go *there!* "Let your light shine before others, so that they may see your good works and give glory to your Father in heaven" (Matthew 5:16 NRSV).

> Do not be afraid of those who kill the body but cannot kill the soul. Rather, be afraid of the One who can destroy both soul and body in hell. Are not two sparrows sold for a penny? Yet not one of them will fall to the ground apart from the will of your Father. And even the very hairs of your head are all numbered. So don't be afraid; you are worth more than many sparrows. (Matthew 10:28-31)

Cling to the promises of Scripture. Take a risk and live as if they were true, *for they are.* Courage comes in doing a brave thing.

EMBARK ON THE LIFELONG JOURNEY OF SPIRITUAL FORMATION AND RENOVATION

It's not by sheer will that we become brave. It takes reformation of the heart. God doesn't call us to *try* to be brave but to *train* to be brave. We won't arrive at it tomorrow, but hopefully, by the grace of God, we'll be more brave ten years from now. Three resources that have been very helpful for me and my IJM colleagues are Dallas Willard's *Divine Conspiracy* and *Renovation of the Heart,* and John Ortberg's *The Life You've Always Wanted.*

God honors the earnest intent of our heart and dignifies our existence with real choices. And in presenting before us the struggle for justice, our Maker asks: Do you want to be brave, or do you want to be safe? Jesus wants us to realize that it's a choice, and he wants to help us make the joyful choice. Most importantly, Jesus wants us to know that he takes care of us so well that it is actually safe to be brave.

Remember what Lucy said in *The Lion, the Witch and the Wardrobe* when she hears of Aslan for the first time? She asks, "Is he quite safe?" The answer, of course, is, "No, he's not safe, but he's good." Even so, as we follow such a lion into the world, it will not be safe. But it will be good. Very good.

Would You Rather Be
Safe or Brave?

RECENTLY, ONE OF THE GREATEST JOYS of my life has been the opportunity to coach peewee contact football. By *peewee,* I mean boys that are seven, eight and nine years old. By *contact* football, I mean these kids put on the full gear (helmets, shoulder pads and mouth guards) and try to knock each other down, hard. It's great fun.

One of the most fascinating moments of peewee contact football occurs very early in the season. It is the magic moment when the brand new peewee discovers that contact football is about *contact.* The peewee has seen football on TV and may think it's about a party in a big stadium. And after listening to the announcers, the colorful commentators and the adults in the room, he may think football is about how smart you can be in analyzing the game. Then he comes to the first week of conditioning practice before the equipment is handed out—and he can think it's about running fast, dodging cones and catching passes.

Then finally—oh, finally—he is issued his shiny helmet, broad shoulder pads and dazzling new jersey. He takes the equipment home to show his family and dashes down the street to show his best friend. At this stage the glories of the gear seem quite enough; football is about the uniform. Then the first day of contact practice finally rolls around, and the new peewee finds himself in a series of shocking and intentional collisions for which no one is apologizing. Shortly thereafter the magic epiphany occurs, and the peewee discovers what football is about—*contact.*

At such a moment, the new peewee is forced to make a decision: does he really want to be a football player or not? But sometimes peewees need help in clarifying the choice. In fact, I remember when my mother helped me to decide.

Riding home from one of my early contact practices as a new peewee, I told my mom I'd had enough. I didn't want to go to practice anymore. Knowing a thing or two about her eight-year-old, my mom simply said, "Oh"—and then after letting me sit for a spell in the absence of enthusiastic affirmation of my decision, she said, "Well, I suppose you can turn in your uniform and equipment to the coach tomorrow." This suggestion was, of course, horrifying to me—after all, I *loved* football. I certainly loved the *idea* of football—and I certainly looked fabulous in the uniform. I was thinking maybe I could just be the kind of football player who wore the uniform but didn't do all that contact stuff. My mom, however, helped me see that the contact stuff was precisely what football was about. After she encouraged me past the shock of the first few bumps, I found out I really was a football player because I truly loved what football was about: contact.

It might have been sweet of my mom to let me avoid the bumps and bruises of the practices and games, and just hold on to the uniform, *pretending* to be a football player. She could have acted like it was possible to both be a football player and avoid the contact of football—to pretend that a choice wasn't required.

But that wouldn't be true, and thankfully she loved me more profoundly than that. Gloriously, she allowed me to discover one of the great, authentic joys of my childhood. Good parents, I think, help their kids clarify the reality of life's choices.

CLARIFYING THE CHOICES

God, our heavenly Father, is a good parent. And he likewise loves us deeply enough to clarify the important choices of life. This isn't always easy for me to hear, but I'm so glad he doesn't withhold the best by failing to tell me the truth.

And here is one choice that our Father wants us to understand as Christians—and I believe this is *the* choice of our age: Do we want to be brave or safe? Gently, lovingly, our heavenly Father wants us to know that we simply can't be both.

On the one hand, all of us carry within us a great yearning to be brave—to be people of courage. Indeed, what is uglier or less attractive to us than cowardice? We admire and exalt the

courageous. We return again and again to litera-
ture and art and cinema to briefly glimpse
the beauty of a brave heart. Indeed, who
wouldn't want to be the kind of person who, when an entire empire
is trembling on its knees before an
idolatrous king, calmly says:

> Do we want to
> be brave or safe? . . .
> We simply can't
> be both.

O Nebuchadnezzar, we do not need to defend ourselves before you in this matter. If we are
thrown into the blazing furnace, the God we serve is able
to save us from it, and he will rescue us from your hand,
O king. But even if he does not, we want you to know, O
king, that we will not serve your gods or worship the image
of gold you have set up. (Daniel 3:16-18)

Wow! I want to be like that. But on the other hand, I don't
want to be like that. I don't ever want to be in a situation in
which I need to be like that. I'd like to be brave, but I'd also like
to be safe. My heavenly Father, however, loves me deeply enough
to tell me the truth. He says I can't be both brave and safe. He
wants me to be clear that I have to decide—and he wants me to
choose to be brave, which means choosing to not be safe.

What does this all mean? What are we supposed to do when
the will of God seems scary?

First we might ask, Is God's will ever supposed to feel scary?
Isn't God supposed to take care of me—isn't he supposed to
keep me from danger and make me safe? I'm probably out of his

will if I am feeling scared, right?

Well, according to Jesus, no. In fact, it turns out that doing God's will in a fallen world is inherently dangerous. Over and over in Scripture Jesus teaches us that his disciples will suffer for following him. Of course, we will *avoid* a lot of suffering *because* we are following him (the suffering of guilt, of self-destruction, of addiction, of hell). But there are other kinds of suffering we will encounter precisely because we *are* following him—and he wants us to be very clear about this. As the apostle Peter taught us:

> Now who will harm you if you are eager to do what is good? But even if you do suffer for doing what is right, you are blessed. . . . Keep your conscience clear, so that, when you are maligned, those who abuse you for your good conduct in Christ may be put to shame. For it is better to suffer for doing good, if suffering should be God's will, than to suffer for doing evil. (1 Peter 3:13-14, 16-17 NRSV)

Clearly, some suffering is a part of God's will. It isn't necessarily the *suffering* itself that is God's will, but rather following the will of God in a fallen world will generate suffering in our lives. There are two things that are always the will of God and almost always dangerous: telling the truth and loving needy people.

In fact, if following Jesus does not feel dangerous, I should probably pause and check to see if it is Jesus I'm following. If I'm playing football and I'm not experiencing much contact, I might check to see if I'm really out on the field. Doing what Jesus does—telling the truth and loving needy people—is inherently unsafe in a fallen world of lies and selfishness.

Let's focus on the dangerous activity to which Jesus invites us: loving needy people. And let's be clear that this is what following Jesus is about. Jesus said all the teaching of the law and the prophets is summed up in the dual command to love God and love our neighbor—especially neighbors in need. In fact, 1 John 4:20 makes it clear that I can't claim to love God, whom I cannot see, if I don't love the neighbors that I do see. If they are in need and I do not respond, the love of God simply isn't in me. Football is about contact—and following Jesus is about loving people in need.

> Doing what Jesus does—telling the truth and loving needy people—is inherently unsafe in a fallen world of lies and selfishness.

It's not safe to love people in need. In fact, I generally try to keep neediness away. Think about those in your family who are most needy, those in your church fellowship who are hurting the most, those on the other side of the city who are most vulnerable. Being with them, serving them and loving them is uncomfortable. It's messy, untidy, unsafe and even dangerous.

And yet, paradoxically, Jesus tells us this is where the deepest joy is found. And based on the experience that my colleagues and I have had at International Justice Mission—it's true. It's not safe, but it's true. At IJM, we specifically try to love those neighbors who are suffering because of violence, abuse and oppression. And it's not safe.

John Richmond

How do you love our neighbors who are enslaved in the rice mills of South Asia (see "The Fight Against Slavery" in chap. 3)? Is it safe?

John Richmond was a young lawyer on the fast track of success with his law firm in Roanoke, Virginia—and then he heard that IJM needed a lawyer to help slaves like Shaibya and her family, who have been locked away as slaves inside a rice mill for three years. Of course, moving his wife and young family to the developing world in order to confront violent slaveholders wasn't safe. But sometimes the will of God is frightening. Indeed, God is asking us to choose between being brave and being safe in order to love those who are hurting.

Not only is loving others not safe, it doesn't look smart.

As John's colleagues and associates heard about his plans to become a full-time abolitionist halfway around the world for IJM, many simply scoffed at him:

- "What do you mean you're going to rescue slaves? It'll never work."
- "You'll walk like a fool into a buzz saw."
- "You'll imperil your family."
- "You'll have no future."
- "You're a fool."

The fact is, when people choose to be brave instead of smart, their courage is generally so threatening to those who are smart rather than brave that they end up being maligned, not congratulated. This is what the Bible says we can expect.

But that's what it takes to show the love of Christ to Shaibya and others held as slaves. So sometimes we have to decide: Are we going to love, or are we going to look smart? Because loving the needy doesn't look smart. And, sadly, in much of our culture this is one of our deepest fears: looking like a fool, naive, unsophisticated, a little too earnest, a loser.

Finally, it's not only unsafe and not smart to try to love people like Shaibya—it also doesn't match the image of the successful.

Generally, there is no wealth and very little regard in helping the needy. Having returned from his term of service overseas, John is neither wealthy nor famous. But then again, Shaibya is no longer a slave. John was able to send his investigators on a daring undercover operation that exposed the terrors inside the rice mill, he mobilized a police raid to rescue the slaves, and he initiated prosecution of the slaveholders. In fact, I've been with Shaibya and the other former slaves as they've shown off their own personal emancipation proclamation certificates documenting that they are no longer slaves but free men and women. John and his aftercare colleagues have secured land and houses and livestock and microloans on which these newly liberated people are building a future of dignity. I've seen it with my own eyes.

And while none of this matches our prevailing cultural descriptions of success, it does match our Savior's definition of significance. According to Christ, significance is found in transforming people's lives through love. This is living a truly significant life.

Occasionally history will validate the significant life that didn't look successful. Few in the 1850s thought, for example, that Harriet Tubman—an illiterate runaway slave who managed to rescue scores of slaves on the underground railroad—was very successful. But now school children across the country mark her life as a model of significance. This makes John Richmond's work all the more amazing; he was able to rescue four times as many slaves as Harriet Tubman. Fortunately, John had the law on his side in a way that Harriet Tubman did not, but someone has to help bring the law to the violent brick factories, rice mills and plantations of South Asia. And by God, John did.

There is overwhelming opportunity for significance in our hurting world. In fact, John and his team have launched the most serious hands-on Christian confrontation with slavery in 150 years. And the work goes on with South Asian leaders that John helped train. Now they carry on the fight in their own community.

Sometimes the will of God is scary because he is asking us to choose between a life that looks successful and a life that is actually significant, between a life that wins the applause of our peers and a life that actually transforms lives through love.

Again, Jesus tried to be as clear as he could about all of this: "For those who want to save their life will lose it, and those who lose their life for my sake will save it" (Luke 9:24 NRSV).

SEAN LITTON

Another colleague of mine, another brilliant lawyer named Sean Litton, calls himself a "mad scientist" of this divine paradox. The hypothesis according to Jesus is this: You find your life when you lose it. So as a proper mad scientist, Sean decided to experiment on himself first. He decided to throw away his life as a fast-track lawyer at an elite national law firm in order to work for IJM. Sean opened our first office in the Philippines, addressing cases of child sexual assault, sex trafficking and illegal detention. Then he decided to include his wife and two kids in the experiment by taking them along. This is how Sean described the experiment:

> IJM needed people to go overseas. I was not so afraid of going as I was of coming back. I was at the top of my profession; I could do anything I wanted. If I went overseas for three or four years to work for some little Christian group, I was sure I would come back to a crappy job, work with crappy people, live in a crappy house, and wear crappy slacks as I drink my crappy coffee while driving my crappy car.
>
> But I just thought, If I can rescue one child from the unspeakable horror of forced prostitution, it would outweigh any sacrifice I could possibly make. How could any sacrifice I make, how could it possibly compare to the daily abuse and suffering of a child locked in a brothel forced to serve four to seven customers a day?

"It was like math," Sean said. "No emotion. I did not have the faith to believe that God could somehow provide for me and that

I might even find joy in it. No, I just expected to be lonely and to suffer. But I signed on to try and save that one child."

And what happened as Sean went to launch our first office in the Philippines, as he ran our office in Thailand and then directed our offices throughout Southeast Asia? God used Sean to lead the rescue of hundreds of women and girls from commercial sexual exploitation and to virtually shut down child prostitution in a city that was once a cesspool of forced child prostitution.

And all of this happened through the power of a very great God working through a very common vessel who made a choice to be brave rather than safe.

What Sean most vividly remembers is not the hundreds of people his teams have served but rather one hurting girl. As Sean put it, "I looked into the eyes of a fifteen-year-old girl who had been brutally raped two years previously and no one had done anything to help her. I was able to tell her, 'God loves you. I know he loves you because he sent me here to help you. I don't know what will happen, but I will fight for you.' " The man who raped her, the son of a police officer, is now serving a twenty-year prison term. The fifteen-year-old girl is now a radiant twenty-year-old woman studying social work in a university so she can help abused children. She actually helps lead IJM's STAR Witness program that helps mentor other child victims of sexual violence on the road to restoration as they confront their perpetrators through the public justice system.

Jesus said, "If you lose your life for my sake, you will find it."

Sean tested the proposition and found Jesus' promise to be true. But he says he almost missed it. So what was holding him back? Four things, he says:

1. Comfort—the state of contented well-being. And we know what this is about: a nice pillow, a couch, air conditioning, a vanilla latte.

2. Security—freedom from danger.

3. Control—having the power over circumstances and events to achieve a desired outcome.

4. Success—the appearance of wealth and the high regard of your peers.

Comfort. Security. Control. Success. These are the four things Sean said he had to let go of in order to get the life that Jesus promised.

According to Sean, he got four things in return:

1. Adventure

2. Faith

3. Miracles

4. Deep knowledge of Jesus

Who among us wouldn't want these?

SAFE OR BRAVE?

Jesus is telling us we have to choose. We can't have adventure, miracles, faith and a deep knowledge of Jesus while holding on to comfort, security, control and success. (Do the math.) Jesus invites us to choose what we really desire.

Where do you and I need to be brave in loving those who are hurting and in need? Perhaps I can make room for such things by offloading some of the other fears and anxieties I carry around. They don't actually have anything to do with loving other people—they have to do with much smaller things.

Are we raising our children to be successful or significant?

Jesus asks parents to make yet another choice. Are we raising our children to be *safe* or to be *brave?* Are we raising our children to be *smart* or to be *loving?* Are we raising them to be *successful* or *significant?* How does God raise his children? In his book *The Problem of Pain,* C. S. Lewis made an observation that is worth lingering over. "Love," Lewis wrote, "is something more stern and splendid than mere kindness. . . . Kindness merely as such cares not whether its object becomes good or bad, provided only that it escapes suffering."

My vulnerabilities as a parent are such that sometimes I simply want my kids to escape suffering. But if I keep them completely safe, they will never have a chance to be truly good or brave. Is that what I want?

One of the greatest privileges of being at IJM over these last ten years has been to watch hundreds of young, talented, passionate interns serve with us. They dramatically advance the mission with their intelligence, their hard work and their authenticity. They inspire me and my colleagues immensely. Interestingly, through the IJM internship program I have also had the opportunity to connect with hundreds of intern parents. It has been absolutely fascinating to watch these wonderful, earnest Christian parents respond to their own children's radical courage in following Christ. For many, it is one of the most difficult experiences of their Christian faith.

We recruit hundreds of these Christian young people at the top of their game and send them off to very tough places to go serve needy and hurting people. This is, of course, a tough step of faith for these young people, but it is a traumatizing leap of faith for their parents. For twenty-plus years these parents have been plowing the faith and love of Jesus into their children. And then shockingly, their sons and daughters turn around and start acting as if it's all actually true. They simply go and do it! And their parents struggle. Most struggle really well—but I think all are surprised by how unprepared they are for the test.

I believe there comes a time when our children rightly ask, "Mom and Dad, why are you giving me all this stuff?"

After we have poured into our children all the good food and shelter and clothing, after we have provided them with great education, discipline, structure and love, after we have worked so hard to provide every good thing, they turn to us and ask, "Why have you given all this to me?"

And the honest answer from me is, "So you'll be safe."

And my kid looks up at me and says, "Really? That's it? You want me to be safe? Your grand ambition for me is that nothing bad happens?"

And I think something inside them dies. They either go away to perish in safety, or they go away looking for adventure in the wrong places. Jesus, on the other hand, affirms their sense of adventure and their yearning for larger glory. In fact, he is encouraging us to affirm this calling in our children and to raise them up to be brave, to be loving and to be significant. But honestly, sometimes I just want my kids to be safe. And I think they smell my fear, and it builds little prisons that can last a lifetime.

According to Jesus, it doesn't have to be that way. He gives me a role in helping my kids choose to be brave, to be loving and to be significant. In the end, this is the stuff that will change the world.

FOLLOWING JESUS

However, before I can lead others, Jesus knows I must make a choice for myself. He is inviting all of us on his great, costly expedition of transformation in the world—but we must respond. Are we coming or staying? Jesus is relentlessly issuing the invitation and forcing a choice to action. What are we going to *do?* I am much more interested in telling Jesus and others what I *believe*, but Jesus (and the watching world) knows that what I truly believe will be manifested in what I choose to *do.*

For many of us the boundary of our range of action is determined by our ultimate fears. Of course, we prefer not to think of ourselves as limited by fear. And our fears often remain hidden (even from ourselves) right up to the very moment when we must *act*. Then, what we actually believe determines what we are able to do. In fact, as Jesus' time on earth drew to a close, he was increasingly blunt about this: words weren't enough; actions identified those who truly believed in him.

Many people admired, were attracted to, and wanted to be with and blessed by Jesus. But Jesus chose those who trusted him so much that they would drop everything to follow him. Some of the saddest pictures in the Gospels are of those who liked Jesus but couldn't trust him enough to follow him.

One of the most powerful and arresting stories in this vein is the story of "The Rich Ruler," as many Bible versions label it. This subhead is unfortunate because it leads most of us to think the story doesn't have anything to do with us. After all, we're not rulers, we wouldn't consider ourselves rich, and we'd never claim that we had obeyed all the commandments, as he did. Accordingly, I always pictured this spoiled and sanctimonious boy-king who gets his comeuppance when Jesus shows him to be the greedy sinner he really is. I thought this until I carefully read the story, and then what I mostly saw was *me*.

Looking at the Gospel texts (the story is found in Matthew 19:16-30; Mark 10:17-30; Luke 18:18-30) I find a devout believer who adores Jesus. According to Luke, he is a man of some

unspecified authority or leadership in the community. Neverthe-
less, when it comes to Jesus, his posture is one of utter humility.
He literally runs to see Jesus. Pompous, self-important authorities don't run to see anybody. And this earnest young man not
only runs, he kneels before Jesus. He addresses Jesus with titles
of great reverence for his day: "Good master" or "Good teacher."
His heart and mind are directed toward the ultimate question of
eternal salvation, and he thinks Jesus has the answer. Jesus points
the young man back to what he already knows about obeying the
law, and the young man says (in front of all his neighbors, who
would know) that since he was a young boy he has been careful
not to murder or commit adultery, to be honest and to honor his
parents. Does Jesus rebuke him for his arrogant self-righteousness?
No. On the contrary, after the young man answers Jesus, the
Bible says, "Jesus looked at him and loved him" (Mark 10:21). He
loved him. Jesus didn't roll his eyes or incite others to laugh. He
"looked at him" and "loved him."

But this earnest, extraordinarily devout believer is restless.
He feels he has done what his religious tradition has taught him
to do, but in the presence of Jesus it just doesn't feel satisfying.
In fact, after affirming his compliance with the basics of the law,
the young man asks, "What do I still lack?" (Matthew 19:20).
He knows his own personal piety is not enough. He knows there
must be more to truly enter the kingdom of God. The young
man asked the question, so Jesus cuts to the chase. He takes the
young man right up to his particular boundary of fear and invites

him to cross it: "If you want to be perfect," Jesus replies, "go, sell your possessions and give to the poor, and you will have treasure in heaven. Then come, follow me" (Matthew 19:21).

In one of the most starkly sad moments recorded in Scripture, the earnest young man, presented with the chance to truly follow the Maker and Redeemer of the world, finds he has too much to lose. He walks away grieving. Why? Because he wants to follow Jesus. But he can't, because he is afraid of what it will cost him.

It turns out he really doesn't believe that Jesus is good—that is to say, that Jesus is *the* good, the ultimate good. At first, it seems like the devout young man thought Jesus was good, because he addressed Jesus as "Good teacher." However, Jesus knows it's not what we say, but what we *do*. So he asks him. "Why do you call me good? No one is good—except God alone." If Jesus is truly almighty God and the ultimate good, then it is the most fantastic bargain to abandon everything else and follow him. Indeed, if quizzed, the reverent young man would probably answer correctly: Of course, the kingdom of heaven is like treasure hidden in a field, and anyone who finds it would *joyfully* sell all to buy that field. But it is Jesus' call to *action*—to actually sell all he has—that reveals his deepest fear about the cost of following Jesus, and it's just too scary.

I vividly remember when I finally had to make the decision to abandon my career at the U.S. Department of Justice to become the first employee of a not-for-profit organization that didn't yet actually exist called International Justice Mission. I had worked for three years with friends on the *idea* of IJM and was very excited, in theory, about this dream of following Jesus in the work of justice in the world. But then I had to actually *act*. I had to walk into the Department of Justice and turn in my badge. This was unsettling. Accordingly, I tried to be both very brave and very safe. That is to say, I walked in and asked my bosses for a yearlong *leave of absence*. That way, if this whole not-for-profit thing didn't work, I could get my job back. No harm done. Failing to see my unique value to the U.S. Department of Justice, however, my bosses politely declined.

Now, at the very threshold of all I had prayed and worked for, I was suddenly feeling very nervous. Indeed, the demand that I actually cut loose my career forced me to confront what I really believed about this adventure, and to confront my fears. What was I really afraid of? As I thought about it, I feared humiliation. If my little justice ministry idea didn't work, no one was going to die. If IJM turned out be a bad idea and collapsed, my kids weren't going to starve. We'd probably just have to live with my parents for a while until I could find another job, but with my education, odds are I would soon find a job. The fact is, I would be terribly embarrassed. Having told everybody about my great idea, they would know that it was a bad idea or that I was a bad leader. Either way, it would be humiliating.

So there it was. My boundary of fear. I sensed God inviting me to an extraordinary adventure of service, but deep inside I was

afraid of looking like a fool and a loser. This was actually very helpful to see, because it helped me get past it. When I am fifty, do I
really want to look back and say, *Yeah, I sensed that God was calling
me to lead a movement to bring rescue to people who desperately need an
advocate in the world, but I was afraid of getting embarrassed and so I never
even tried?* Putting it so starkly was empowering. That wasn't who I
wanted to be, and it wasn't who I had to be. If Je-
sus was extending the invitation, my job was to
seize it; it was his job to make it succeed,
or not. I could let Jesus be the deciding
factor, not my fear.

Fear is normal, even among the earnest and devout, and it can be overcome.

This is the journey I have seen time
and again in the struggle for justice. Fear
is normal, even among the earnest and devout, and it can be overcome. But first we must
see the opportunity it provides—a revelation that only comes as
we step to the precipice of action.

As it turns out, it's quite possible to be very earnest and also be
afraid. As the Gospel story of the devout young man makes clear,
it's possible to run to Jesus in humble adoration and to bow at his
feet in worship, and yet at the same time be fearful that the cost
of following him is too great—because we really don't believe he
will take care of us in the end. Yet, we are unlikely to see our fundamental fears until we are called to act. This is why Jesus is so
relentless in his invitations to action. He wants us to completely
trust him, to walk in the freedom and power and joy that comes

from authentically believing that all will be well in following the all-good and almighty God. Jesus is very explicit about this. After the young man left, Jesus says to those disciples who are willing to follow him: "I tell you the truth, no one who has left home or wife or brothers or parents or children for the sake of the kingdom of God will fail to receive many times as much in this age and, in the age to come, eternal life" (Luke 18:29-30).

Clearly, the young man, who has many possessions, just can't bring himself to trust Jesus on this one—and that's very sad.

Why does Jesus call the devout young man to such demanding action? Is it to expose him as a fraud? No, there is no evidence of this. Again, just before he makes the costly invitation, the text says that "Jesus looked at him and loved him." Jesus loves the young man so much that he wants to show him the boundaries of unnecessary fear that is robbing him of true freedom and joy. No doubt Jesus also wanted some poor people to receive the aid that would flow from the young man's philanthropy. But the text is clear. Jesus loves the young man and wants him to follow Jesus on a path that leads to a place where he will get eternal life *and* a hundred times more than he may lose. Jesus knows the young man's boundary of fear and wants to set him free.

CROSSING BOUNDARIES

Jesus likewise loves us. He also knows our particular boundaries of fear and wants to set us free. This is why he invites us to follow him in the demanding struggle for justice. There is a boundary of fear that is keeping us in our cul-de-sac, and he knows that deep down we want to get out. He sees us restless but trapped, and he loves us. He wants to reveal that hidden boundary to us, and he knows that the call to justice is precisely and mysteriously calibrated to expose our fear. More deeply than we can imagine, he longs for us to see the boundary, to take his hand and step over it. Jesus' mission of justice is certainly the way he shows his love for those who are being abused, but just as much, the expedition is for us.

> Seek justice,
>> rescue the oppressed,
> defend the orphan,
>> plead for the widow. (Isaiah 1:17 NRSV)

This is the expedition that brings freedom to both those who follow and those who are found.

> If you spend yourselves in behalf of the hungry
>> and satisfy the needs of the oppressed,
>> then your light will rise in the darkness,
>> and your night will become like the noonday.
> The LORD will guide you always;
>> he will satisfy your needs in a sun-scorched land
>> and will strengthen your frame.
>> You will be like a well-watered garden,
>> like a spring whose waters never fail. (Isaiah 58:10-11)

And Jesus says, "Come, follow me."

Appendix 1

Partnering with International Justice Mission

THIS APPENDIX COMPRISES PRACTICAL NEXT STEPS for individuals and churches who desire to partner with International Justice Mission as it seeks justice, rescues the oppressed, defends the orphan and pleads for the widow (Isaiah 1:17).

Please visit our website at www.ijm.org to acquire the resources mentioned in the appendix.

EDUCATE

One advocate for every slave. Text or e-mail this question to a friend: Did you know there are 27 million slaves in the world today? If they have questions, encourage them to search the Internet using these words: *National Geographic, September 2003, Slavery.*

Sending a text or e-mail might seem like a small act, but if we are able to convince a mere 10 percent of the U.S. population to be concerned about modern-day slavery, we would end up with one advocate for every slave in the world. Imagine harnessing the power of 27 million people committed to the abolition of slavery. It would change the course of history.

Whether you are interested in seeing an end to slavery, sexual violence, theft of land from orphans and widows, or illegal detention, it all begins with awareness.

Awareness creates the social demand necessary to bring change. Can you imagine 27 million people calling their representatives in Washington, D.C., to discuss how we might end slavery in our lifetime? It would dramatically change the political landscape.

Awareness also helps raise the resources necessary for growth. The two greatest needs for IJM to expand its mission are qualified professionals to join the team full-time and financial resources so IJM can continue to show up in the places where the poor simply don't have an advocate. Without increasing awareness, the growth of justice ministry will be limited.

Next steps. Join us in educating your church, family, friends and coworkers about injustice and the work of International Justice Mission. Visit the IJM website for world-class video and print resources to share with others and to assist with group presentations.

Justice Generation. In the last fifty years we have seen a shift in the North American church that has resulted in the emergence of many Christian relief and development agencies dedicated to the ministry of mercy and compassion. In the last ten to fifteen

years we began to see a shift in the North American church re-
garding Christians' beliefs about the need and opportunity to be
engaged in justice ministry. I believe God is moving the body of
Christ more deeply into his heart to bring justice for those suffering from violent oppression.

The coming generation is positioned to have the greatest im-
pact in continuing to bring about this shift. In fact, we often
discover in speaking at youth events that those in attendance already have a conviction that God seeks justice for the oppressed.
As a result, we refer to them as the "Justice Generation." It is our
desire to nurture this God-given passion in the coming generation, but we need your assistance.

Next steps. Connect International Justice Mission with your
church youth or your community. To learn more, view the youth
resources on our website.

If you are a student, you will notice that some of the resources
that have been developed were generated by your peers. Check
out what is available from our website, but also consider what
you might envision among your friends to seek justice.

EXPLORE

IJM mission training. Add a justice edge to any mission experience. Churches often send short-term teams to the developing
world to build homes, work with orphanages, engage people in
evangelism and so forth. IJM has a training DVD that can equip
any type of mission team to identify injustice issues while in the

field. This will give the team insight on what questions to ask, where to visit and what to look for.

Identifying injustice issues in the communities your team serves provides a holistic picture of what God desires for that community. In the process, the team might discover an injustice issue that the church can assist with.

Next steps. Visit the IJM website to acquire the IJM Mission Training DVD. Once you review the training, we encourage you to speak with the leadership of your church to see how this tool might enable the church to add a justice edge to the missions program.

IJM Institute. The IJM Institute is a web-based community where Christian leaders share ideas and engage in dialogue about how to overcome injustice. It is a source for leaders to gain free access to cutting-edge tools, best practices and theological re-flection as they seek to draw others into the work of justice.

Next steps. To join the IJM Institute, visit www.ijminstitute .org. Take a moment to consider three to four other Christian leaders you would like to invite to join this dynamic community. Send them a personal note to share your reasons for applying, and give them the web address so they can check it out as well.

ENGAGE

Seek God. In confronting violent oppression, we are aware of our limitations. We are desperate for God's assistance to move the cases forward and to protect victims and IJM staff who are on the front lines. As a result, IJM staff around the world stop work each day at 11 a.m. to gather for corporate prayer.

We would love to have you as a partner in seeking God for assistance. You can receive weekly prayer requests from IJM related to specific cases and join us for an annual Global Prayer Gathering in Washington, D.C.

The Global Prayer Gathering is a unique event in the life of IJM. It is the one time when we have all the IJM field directors in Washington, D.C., to share firsthand stories of rescue as well as the current challenges they are facing. It's a time when all IJM prayer partners and supporters are invited to gather with us for a focused time of prayer and worship as we ask God to intervene on behalf of the victims of injustice throughout the world. We have seen remarkable answers to prayer through this time together. Please join us in this powerful event.

Next steps. Visit the IJM website to sign up to partner with International Justice Mission in prayer and for registration information for the next Global Prayer Gathering. Take a moment to share IJM's mission with those who love to pray. Give them our web address so they can explore how they might align their passion for prayer with God's desire to seek justice for the oppressed.

Become a Freedom Partner. By giving a monthly gift of $50, you can enable International Justice Mission to stand up, speak up and show up on behalf of the oppressed. Every person has the capacity to help bring a miracle in the lives of those who suffer injustice.

As a Freedom Partner you select where to invest your monthly gift—either in a region where IJM does casework or to overcome a specific injustice, such as sex trafficking. IJM will provide rescue stories and consistent updates from the area you choose to invest in.

Next steps. To become a Freedom Partner, visit the IJM website and click on "Take Action." Your investment will result in high returns—an advocate showing up, a victim set free and perpetrators held accountable for their abuse.

Model churches. What does it look like for a church to incorporate justice into their global witness? We have been blessed with wonderful church partners that have been pioneers in this neglected area of missions. To give you a few examples, churches have (1) explored injustice issues in countries where they are deeply invested in missions, (2) introduced IJM staff to key leaders around the world, (3) sent professionals to work with our field offices, (4) provided valuable research for the IJM team and (5) helped pay for the rescue the poor cannot afford.

Next steps. To help paint a picture of church partnership, we have posted stories of churches on our website that we consider models of seeking justice. You will also find contact information on the website so you can speak with our church mobilization team. The team can assist as you explore bringing an IJM speaker to your church and practical steps for moving your church to model church status.

Just representation. The U.S. government has significant capacity to influence world leaders in the area of human rights abuse. As an example, IJM worked with other organizations and congressional leaders to establish a mechanism to assess the degree to which countries are fighting human trafficking and for this assessment to be one of the factors in considering foreign aid.

More could be accomplished, but to do this we need your assistance. For U.S. leaders, it is critical that they know people from their constituency care about global issues of injustice. As you can imagine, they receive a lot of feedback from constituents about domestic concerns. There needs to be an equally strong voice for the United States to be a champion of the global poor who are being consistently and horrifically abused.

Next steps. Visit the IJM website and click on "Get Involved" to review strategies and opportunities to engage your representatives on justice issues. All the issues are bipartisan and are intended for all to participate together as one voice for the oppressed.

Global church. It is vital for IJM to have the local church in the developing world at the forefront of the justice movement. Their communities are affected by the violence, and out of their congregations God will create the social demand for change, raise up leaders to join the IJM team and give us connections with Christians who are in positions of influence.

Next steps. IJM continues to hire church mobilization staff for its field offices worldwide to build bridges with local churches and church leaders. Please visit the IJM website to view job openings and opportunities to unite the global church. We seek the names of overseas church leaders who are eager to partner in IJM's mission.

Career in human rights. As a rapidly growing organization, IJM has a constant need for qualified interns, fellows and full-time professionals.

For college students, graduate students, law school students and recent graduates, IJM has a top-notch internship program. It is a wonderful opportunity to explore a career in human rights through hands-on experience and a mentoring relationship with one of the IJM staff.

IJM has a fellowship program for professionals interested in volunteering for an extended time in one of our field offices, and we have a constant need for qualified professionals interested in seeking justice full time.

In addition to lawyers and criminal investigators, we also need professionals in other disciplines such as management, administration, IT, donor relations, communications, social work and accounting.

Next steps. To review detailed information on the internship and fellowship programs as well as to review current job openings, visit the IJM website. In addition to considering how God might be speaking to you, consider who you know who might be a good fit for IJM. It would be a great blessing to us if you would take a moment to send an e-mail or place a call to a few people to let them know about the opportunities to volunteer and work at IJM.

Appendix 2

Further Resources

THE FOLLOWING ARE SOME ORGANIZATIONS that can offer more information on trafficking, slavery and other violent forms of oppression.

Amnesty International

www.amnesty.org

Anti-Slavery International (U.K.)

www.antislavery.org

Freedom House

www.freedomhouse.org

HumanTrafficking.org

www.humantrafficking.org

Human Rights First

www.humanrightsfirst.org

Human Rights Watch

www.hrw.org

International Labour Organization

www.ilo.org

UNICEF

United Nations Children's Fund

www.unicef.org

UNIFEM

United Nations Development Fund for Women

www.unifem.org

U.S. Department of Justice

www.usdoj.gov

U.S. Department of Health & Human Services

The Campaign to Rescue & Restore Victims of Human Trafficking

www.acf.hhs.gov/trafficking/index.html

U.S. Department of State

Office to Monitor and Combat Trafficking in Persons

www.state.gov/g/tip

World Health Organization

www.who.int/en

Questions for Discussion and Reflection

Chapter 1: Going on the Journey but Missing the Adventure

1. Have you ever gone on the trip but missed the adventure? What happened, and how did you feel afterward?

2. How would you respond to John Stuart Mill's indictment of Christians, that "whenever conduct is concerned, they look round for Mr. A and B to direct them how far to go in obeying Christ"?

3. Have you ever found yourself calculating the limits of your obedience? What did you discover?

4. Do you do work that requires you to stop every thirty minutes to ask for God's help? What do you imagine your daily life would look like if you did this?

5. When have you stepped out in faith, had a desperate need and seen God's provision?

Chapter 2: From Rescued to Rescuer

1. Do you resonate with the author's sense that there is a discontent among many Christians today, and that many of us are still at the visitor's center? Do you feel this is true in your own life?

2. Have you found yourself asking, "Now what?" What were the circumstances and what did you do?

3. If it is true that "our rescue is not the ultimate destination," what is?

4. The author proposes three reasons for why we settle for less than the best God has to offer us: ignorance, despair and fear. Of these three, which do you identify with most? Why?

5. Recount a time when you stepped out beyond your comfort zone in a way that required courage. What might it look like to live that way on a daily basis? What is getting in the way?

Chapter 3: The Surprising Path to Courage

1. When have you tried to fashion your own path and discovered that you were wrong, that God had a different path for you? Explain.

2. Do you agree with the author that "the struggle for justice in [God's] world . . . is a call to all his people," and that "the work of justice is no less fundamental in Christ's call to discipleship" than evangelizing and caring for our neighbors? Why or why not?

3. The author declares that "sometimes the biblical call to justice

feels like it should be declared 'void for vagueness.' " And "it is . . . discouraging when [we] can't picture what [justice] means or how [we can] actually do it." From this chapter, describe what justice means. Give some concrete examples identified by the author.

4. How is the ministry of justice different from the ministries of evangelism and compassion? Where do these three ministries mentioned by both Micah and Jesus overlap?

5. What are the three secrets IJM has learned about violence in our world today, and how can we stop it?

6. How would you define the biblical call for Christians to seek justice?

Chapter 4: The God of Justice

1. When have you felt a stinging sense of injustice? How did you respond?

2. Name some people or groups who claim "slogans of justice." How have they influenced your view of justice?

3. If "justice is not optional for Christians," what are some ways that you can be involved in a ministry of justice right now?

Chapter 5: Just Worship

1. As you read this chapter, what was your response to all the Scriptures that stress the importance of justice to your worship?

2. What guideposts from the Bible have you used to guide your life? Which have been the best?

3. What can you do to encourage others to live lives of justice that are pleasing to God?

4. What are some ways that your church encourages its members to actively pursue justice?

Chapter 6: Loving God and Our Neighbor

1. Think of a time when you felt that you were being treated unjustly. Share what the situation was and how it made you feel.

2. Do you think it's true that the importance of justice to worship "has been marginalized in most of our churches over the last hundred years"? Why or why not?

3. List three or four examples in history where great injustices have been exposed and justice prevailed.

4. Do you believe that the average Christian can do something about injustice around the world? Explain.

Chapter 7: Charging the Darkness

1. What do you think compelled William, Donaldina and Irena to seek justice when others who undoubtedly knew about injustice didn't act?

2. Recount the story of at least one other hero of the faith who has "charged the darkness" of injustice for Christ.

3. Has there been a time when you saw someone else charge the darkness and it gave you the courage to follow? When was it, and what happened?

4. Have you yourself charged the darkness and inspired someone to do the same? Explain.

Chapter 8: The Witness of One

1. Recount a time when you were desperate to help someone you love, but you couldn't. How did you feel? Who eventually helped? What was the outcome? What could you do differently in the future?

2. Have you ever had the chance to help someone facing injustice? If so, explain what happened.

Chapter 9: Seizing the Gift of Courage

1. We often fear that our life isn't significant apart from the quality and quantity of our things. Thus, the author says, much of our "hard-charging activity" is generated by "nervous energy" to overcome this fear. Can you relate to this? What ways can you see your Christian activity being generated by fear?

2. According to the author, "our stuff, our reputation, our standing, our children, our ideology and our investments" are meant to be "put at risk" for Christ. What was your reaction when you read this? Explain.

3. The author suggests that while Christ (Aslan) is good, he is not

safe. What do you think he meant by this?

4. What are three or four practical ways you can train to be brave?

Chapter 10: Would You Rather Be Safe or Brave?

1. Have you ever suffered for the cause of Christ? If so, what was the source of your suffering? What was the result?

2. Do you believe it is true that "some suffering is a part of God's will"? Why or why not?

3. Would you rather be safe or brave? Explain.

4. The author says many Christians are primarily interested in comfort, security, control and success. Do you agree or disagree? Why?

5. What would it take for you to give up your present job or life situation to work for justice in an organization such as International Justice Mission?

Acknowledgments

I AM GRATEFUL TO MY PAST AND PRESENT COLLEAGUES at International Justice Mission, who time and again have chosen to be brave. Several of them are featured in this book—among them Sharon Cohn Wu, Sean Litton, Blair Burns, John Richmond and Kaign Christy. They are joined by many attorneys, investigators, social workers, support staff and administrators around the world who are boldly seeking justice on behalf of the oppressed. Many offered assistance and encouragement in the completion of this book, including Bill Clark, Pamela Livingston, Bethany Hoang, Larry Martin, Kate Cooper, Betsy Hutson and Ruthie McGinn.

I am especially grateful to my Father and my God for the privilege of knowing, working, laughing and praying with my dear departed brother Colonel Clement Mudenda. As the director of IJM's Zambia Field Office, our Colonel showed us just how powerful the gentleness and justice of Jesus can be.

Finally, to my wife, Jan, I am so thankful for the sheltering tree of grace from which all expeditions of courage proceed and return.

INTERNATIONAL
JUSTICE MISSION.

"All that is necessary for the triumph of evil
is that good men do nothing."

EDMUND BURKE

For more information about how you can get
involved in the work of justice, please contact
International Justice Mission:

P.O. Box 58147

Washington, D.C. 20037-8147

703-465-5495

www.ijm.org